HUMOUR

Terry Eagleton is distinguished visiting professor of English literature, University of Lancaster, and the author of more than fifty books in the fields of literary theory, postmodernism, politics, ideology and religion.

T0016294

HUMOUR

TERRY EAGLETON

YALE UNIVERSITY PRESS
NEW HAVEN AND LONDON

Copyright © 2019 Yale University

First published in paperback in 2022

For information about this and other Yale University Press publications, please contact:
U.S. Office: sales.press@yale.edu   yalebooks.com
Europe Office: sales@yaleup.co.uk   yalebooks.co.uk

Set in Adobe Garamond Regular by IDSUK (DataConnection) Ltd
Printed in Great Britain by Clays Ltd, Elcograf S.p.A

Library of Congress Control Number: 2019931197

ISBN 978-0-300-24314-7 (hbk)
ISBN 978-0-300-25502-7 (pbk)

A catalogue record for this book is available from the British Library.

10 9 8 7 6 5 4 3 2 1

For Trevor Griffiths

CONTENTS

PREFACE

A good many studies of humour begin with the shamefaced acknowledgement that to analyse a joke is to kill it dead. This is not in fact true. It is true that if you want to raise a laugh it is unwise to joke and dissect your joke at the same time, rather as some US presidents are said to have been unable to walk and chew gum simultaneously; but there are not many comedians who come up with a theoretical inquiry into their wisecracks at the very moment they are delivering them. Those who do so are generally to be found in job centres, not in clubs and theatres. (There are, to be sure, exceptions, such as the brilliantly original comedian Stewart Lee, who deconstructs his own comedy as he goes along and analyses the audience's response to it.) Otherwise, humour and the analysis of humour are perfectly capable of coexisting. Knowing how a joke works does not necessarily sabotage it, any more than knowing how a poem works ruins it.

In this as in other matters, theory and practice occupy different spheres. An anatomical acquaintance with the large intestine is no obstacle to enjoying a meal. Gynaecologists can lead fulfilling sex lives, while obstetricians can coo over babies. Astronomers confronted every day with the utterly insignificant status of the Earth within the universe do not hit the bottle or leap off a cliff, or at least not for that reason.

There are, to be sure, a number of remarkably humourless accounts of humour on the library shelves. Some such studies come thickly furnished with graphs, charts, diagrams, statistics and reports of laboratory experiments.[1] One glum trio of scientific researchers even appear to cast doubt on whether jokes actually exist. There are, however, some illuminating commentaries as well, a range of which I have drawn upon in this book. Theories of humour can be as useful as theories of polygamy or paranoia as long as they are marked by a certain intellectual modesty. Like any fruitful hypothesis, they need to acknowledge their own limits. There will always be anomalous cases, unresolved puzzles, awkward consequences, inconvenient implications and the like. Theories can be riddled with discrepancies and still perform some productive work, rather as a fuzzy photograph of someone can be better than no photograph at all, and a job worth doing is usually worth doing badly. The incomparable William Hazlitt quotes a fellow author, Isaac Barrow, as observing that humour is so 'versatile and multiform', a phenomenon of which any exhaustive definition is impossible to come by:

Sometimes it is lodged in a sly question, in a smart answer, in a quirkish reason, in a shrewd intimation, in cunningly diverting or cleverly restoring an objection; sometimes it is couched in a bold scheme of speech, in a tart irony, in a lusty hyperbole, in a startling metaphor, in a plausible reconciliation of contradictions, or in acute nonsense . . . a mimical look or gesture passeth for it; sometimes an affected simplicity, sometimes a presumptuous bluntness giveth it being; sometimes it riseth only from a lucky hitting upon what is strange: sometimes from a crafty wresting obvious matter to the purpose; often it consisteth in one knows not what, and springeth up one can hardly tell how . . . It is, in short, a manner of speaking out of the simple and plain way . . . which by a pretty surprising uncouthness in conceit or expression doth affect and amuse the fancy, shewing in it some wonder and breathing some delight thereto.[2]

It would be a foolhardy theorist who would seek to cram all that into a single formula. Even so, humour is not simply an enigma, any more than poetry is. It is possible to say something relatively cogent and coherent about why we laugh, though whether I have done so in these pages is up to the reader to judge.

T.E.

2017

1

ON LAUGHTER

They laughed when I told them I wanted to be a comedian. Well they're not laughing now.

Bob Monkhouse

Laughter is a universal phenomenon, which is not to say a uniform one. In an essay entitled 'The Difficulty of Defining Comedy', Samuel Johnson remarks that though human beings have been wise in many different ways, they have always laughed in the same way, but this is surely doubtful. Laughter is a language with a host of different idioms: cackling, chortling, grunting, chuckling, shrieking, bellowing, screaming, sniggering, gasping, shouting, braying, yelping, snickering, roaring, tittering, hooting, guffawing, snorting, giggling, howling, screeching and so on. It can come in blasts, peals, gales, gusts, ripples or torrents, blaring, trumpeting, trickling, swirling or piercing. There are also different ways of smiling, from beaming, smirking and sneering to grinning, leering and simpering. Smiling is visual and laughter primarily aural, but when T. S. Eliot writes in *The Waste Land* of a 'chuckle spread from ear to ear' he fuses the two phenomena.

Chortling, sniggering and so on denote different physical modes of laughter, involving as they do such matters as volume, tone, pitch, pace, force, rhythm, timbre and duration. But laughter can also convey a range of emotional attitudes: joyous, sarcastic, sly, raucous, genial, wicked, derisive, dismissive, nervous, relieved, cynical, knowing, smug, lascivious, incredulous, embarrassed, hysterical, sympathetic, skittish, shocked, aggressive or sardonic, not to speak of purely 'social' laughter, which need not express the least amusement.[1] In fact, most of the forms of laughter I have just listed have little or nothing to do with humour. Laughter may be a sign of high spirits rather than amusement, though you are more likely to think things funny if you are feeling euphoric in the first place. Physical modes and emotional attitudes can be combined in a variety of ways, so that you can titter nervously or derisively, bray genially or aggressively, giggle with surprise or delight, cackle appreciatively or sardonically and so on.

The paradox, then, is that though laughter itself is purely a question of the signifier – mere sound without sense – it is socially coded through and through. It is a spontaneous physical occurrence (most of the time, anyway), but one which is socially specific, and as such cusped between nature and culture. Like dance, laughter is a language of the body (Descartes called it an 'inarticulate and explosive cry'),[2] though the body is also enmeshed in meaning of a more conceptual kind. Even so, it will never be entirely at home in that more rarefied sphere. There is always a surplus of brute materiality over sense, and it is this that a lot of humour allows us to savour. It also encourages us to accept this incongruity as natural. Farce in particular tends to dramatise this fateful collision between body and mind.

As a pure enunciation that expresses nothing but itself, laughter lacks intrinsic sense, rather like an animal's cry, but despite this it is richly freighted with cultural meaning. As such, it has a kinship with music. Not only has laughter no inherent meaning, but at its most riotous and convulsive it involves the disintegration of sense, as the body tears one's speech to fragments and the id pitches the ego into temporary disarray. As with grief, severe pain, extreme fear or blind rage, truly uproarious laughter involves a loss of physical self-control, as the body gets momentarily out of hand and we regress to the uncoordinated state of the infant. It is quite literally a bodily disorder. We shall see later that this is one reason why an excess of laughter has frequently been censured as politically dangerous. There is something alarmingly animal about the activity, not least about the kind of noise (hooting, braying, cackling, neighing, bellowing) it involves. It calls to mind our affinity with the other animals – an irony, to be sure, since they do not laugh themselves, or at least not conspicuously so.[3] In this sense, it is at once animal and distinctively human – a miming of the noise of the beasts, yet quite unbestial itself. It is also, of course, one of the most commonplace and pervasive of human pleasures. In *The Book of Laughter and Forgetting*, Milan Kundera quotes the French feminist Annie Leclerc on the subject: 'Bursts of repeated, rushing, unleashed laughter, magnificent laughter, sumptuous and mad . . . laughter of sensual pleasure, sensual pleasure of laughter; to laugh is to live profoundly.'

Laughter signifies, then, but it also involves the breakdown of signification into pure sound, spasm, rhythm and breath. It is hard to form impeccably well-shaped sentences when you are thrashing helplessly around on the floor. The disruption of coherent meaning to be found in so many jokes is reflected in the disintegrative nature of laughter itself. This temporary derangement of meaning is most obvious in the absurd or nonsensical, in goonery and surrealism of one form or another, but it is arguably an aspect of all effective comedy. In one sense, laughter represents the momentary collapse or disruption of the symbolic realm – of the sphere of orderly and articulate meaning – while in another sense it never ceases to rely on it. We do, after all, generally laugh at some object, event, utterance or situation, unless we are simply being tickled, fighting a fit of depression or registering our pleasure in someone's company; and this involves the deployment of concepts, which is one reason why some commentators have claimed that

4

non-linguistic animals do not laugh. Laughter is a form of utterance which springs straight from the body's libidinal depths, but there is a cognitive dimension to it as well. Like fury or envy, it involves beliefs and assumptions. In fact, some forms of humour, as we shall see later, are primarily intellectual affairs. Wit, for example. Farce may convert human action into mere physical motion, but even this depends on moving in a world of meaning. Infants smile almost from birth, but laughter begins only around the third or fourth month, perhaps because of its need to engage the mind.

It is true that laughter can gather an uncontrollable momentum of its own, so that after a while we no longer know exactly what we are laughing at, or laugh simply at the fact that we are laughing. It is what Milan Kundera, quoting Annie Leclerc once more, calls 'laughter so laughable it made us laugh'.[4] There is also the case of contagious laughter, in which we laugh because someone else does, without needing to know what he or she finds so funny. As with certain diseases, you can pick up a dose of laughter without being sure where it came from. Generally speaking, however, laughter alters the mind's relation to the body without suspending it completely.

It is worth noting the curious fact that much of this applies to weeping too.[5] James Joyce speaks in *Finnegans Wake* of 'laughtears', while his compatriot Samuel Beckett writes in *Molloy* of a woman whose dog has just died that 'I thought she was going to cry, it was the thing to do, but on the contrary

5

she laughed. It was perhaps her way of crying. Or perhaps I was mistaken and she was really crying, with the noise of laughter. Tears and laughter, they are so much Gaelic to me.' In fact, laughing and weeping are not always easy to distinguish. Charles Darwin points out in his study of the emotions that laughter can easily be mistaken for grief, and both states may involve copious floods of tears. In *The Naked Ape*, the anthropologist Desmond Morris argues that laughter actually evolved from crying. Laughter, in short, is not always a laughing matter. There have even been lethal epidemics of the stuff in China, Africa, Siberia and elsewhere, hysterical paroxysms in which, so it is alleged, thousands of people have died. In 1962, one such outbreak in what was then Tanganyika immobilised whole school districts for months on end. Since being out of control is never entirely gratifying, laughter can easily border on the unpleasant. Samuel Johnson defines it in his *Dictionary* as 'convulsive merriment', which is not always an agreeable experience. The same is true of being tickled, with its curious blend of the pleasurable and the unbearable. As with watching a horror movie, we are gratified, agitated, excited and uneasy all at the same time. Monkeys who bare their teeth in what appears to be a smile may actually be issuing a threat. Thomas Hobbes writes of laughter in *Leviathan* as a grimace. We speak of people screaming with laughter, gasping for breath, occasionally having a coronary. Lying through his teeth, the narrator of Laurence Sterne's *Tristram Shandy* tells us

6

that he once laughed so hard he broke a blood vessel and lost four pints of blood in two hours. The novelist Anthony Trollope suffered a stroke while laughing at a comic novel, a misfortune by which few of his own readers are likely to be afflicted.[6] Despite its potentially calamitous effects, laughter may be indicative of human progress: only an animal which has learnt to carry objects in its hands rather than its mouth can leave the latter free for chuckling or tittering.

It would be possible to develop a semiotics of laughing or smiling, showing how each genre of laughter or style of facial expression has its place within a complex signifying system. You can, in short, treat laughter as a text, or as a language with so many regional accents. Upper-class Englishmen, for example are more likely to bray than middle-class Englishwomen, who are rather more given to tinkling. There is a style of laughter in Belize that one is unlikely to hear in Belgravia. Military generals tend not to giggle, or popes to cackle. Those who play Santa Claus may beam, but they would be ill advised to snigger. It is hard to imagine Arnold Schwarzenegger simpering, though easy enough to imagine him leering. The president of the World Bank is permitted to laugh heartily but not hysterically.

The ability to assess such modes and tones belongs to what Aristotle calls *phronesis*, meaning our practical social know-how, as is knowing when humour is appropriate or misplaced. For example, one should not recount the joke 'What's black and white and lies on its back in the gutter? – A dead nun' to an elderly nun at prayer in a cathedral, as one of my children did at the age of five. Here is another example of misplaced humour:

Doctor: OK, I've got some good news and some bad news for you.

Patient: Give me the bad news first.

Doctor: The bad news is that you've only got three months to live.

Patient: And the good news?

Doctor: The good news is that I'm just off to Monaco with this unbelievably beautiful woman.

We smile here at the discrepancy between how the brutally jesting or monstrously tactless doctor ought to behave and how he actually does, a tension that is spiced by a spot of agreeable sadism on our part at the expense of the hapless patient. We are gratified by the doctor's sheer chutzpah, his barefaced disregard for both human compassion and professional decorum, which allows us vicariously to indulge our own illicit hankering to be free of such irksome responsibilities. We are relieved for a few moments of the inconvenient burden of compassion. Black humour of this kind eases the guilt we may feel at our glee over the discomfiture of others by socialising it, casting it in the form of a joke to be shared with one's friends and thus rendering it more acceptable.

There is some pleasure to be reaped, too, from laughing in the face of death, and thus being able to make light of our own mortality. To jest at death is to cut it down to size and diminish its fearful power over us, as in another doctor joke:

Patient: How long have I got to live?
Doctor: Ten.
Patient: Ten what? Years? Months? Weeks?
Doctor: No, no: ten, nine, eight, seven . . .

To confront its own extinction in fictional form means that the ego can achieve a momentary transcendence of it, gaining a brief taste of immortality. One thinks of the symbolic victory over death of Woody Allen's grandfather, who as his grandson touchingly reports sold him a watch on his deathbed. Laughter compensates a little for our mortality, as well as for our general infirmity. Indeed, Friedrich Nietzsche remarks that the human animal is the only one to laugh because it suffers so atrociously, and needs to dream up this desperate palliative for its afflictions. Gallows or graveyard humour, however, involves more than a disavowal of death. To cut death down to size with a casual jest is also to vent our spleen on it for the disquiet it causes us.

There is also the question of our unconscious desire for what we fear. What Freud calls *Thanatos* or the death drive pulverises meaning and value, and is thus bound up with that fleeting derangement of sense we know as humour. Like humour, this

9

Dionysian force garbles sense, confounds hierarchies, merges identities, scrambles distinctions and revels in the collapse of meaning, which is why carnival, which accomplishes all this too, is never very far from the cemetery. In cutting the ground from beneath all social distinctions, carnival affirms the absolute equality of all things; but in doing so it sails perilously close to the excremental vision, reducing everything to the sameness of shit. If human bodies are interchangeable in an orgy, so are they in the gas chambers. Dead levelling, as one might call it. Dionysus is the god of drunken revelry and sexual ecstasy, but also a harbinger of death and destruction. The *jouissance* he promises can prove lethal.

The doctor joke, then, grants us some momentary relief from the need to behave with decorum and treat others considerately. It also allows us to stop agonising for a few brief moments over the prospect of death. The notion of humour as a form of relief forms the basis of one widely influential view of it, the so-called release theory. The seventeenth-century philosopher the Earl of Shaftesbury sees comedy as releasing our constrained but naturally free spirits, while Immanuel Kant speaks of laughter in his *Critique of Judgment* as 'an affect resulting from the sudden transformation of a heightened expectation into nothing',[7] which combines the release theory with the concept of incongruity. True to this approach, the Victorian philosopher Herbert Spencer claims that 'mirth is caused by a gush of agreeable feeling which follows the cessation of unpleasant mental strain'.[8]

In *Jokes and Their Relation to the Unconscious*, Sigmund Freud argues that jokes represent a release of the psychic energy we normally invest in maintaining certain socially essential inhibitions.[9] In relaxing such superegoic repression, we save on the unconscious exertion it demands and expend it instead in the form of joking and laughing. It is, so to speak, an economics of humour. On this view, the joke is an impudent smack at the superego. We exult in these Oedipal skirmishes, but conscience and rationality are also faculties we respect, so that a tension is set up between being responsible and running riot. Hegel speaks of the ludicrous in his *Philosophy of Fine Art* as the upshot of a collision between an ungovernable sensual impulse and one's higher sense of duty. It is a conflict reflected in boisterous roars of laughter, which as we have noted already can be as alarming as they are agreeable. Perhaps most jokes betray a murmur of uneasy laughter at the prospect of bringing the Father low. Fearful of being punished for this insolence, our delight at seeing the patriarch dethroned is edged with nervous giggles of guilt, which then spur us to chuckle even more as a defence against this disquiet. If our laughter is edgy, it is because we fear the consequences of this illicit enjoyment as much as we revel in it. This is why we cringe as well as chuckle. The guilt, however, mixes a certain spice into the enjoyment. In any case, we know that the conquest we have chalked up is purely provisional – and a paper victory too, since a joke, after all, is simply a piece of language. We can therefore indulge our iconoclasm while assuaging our guilt about it, secure in the faith that the Father (a figure whom, after all, we love as well as hate) will not be permanently disabled by this minor insurgency. His abject loss of authority is purely temporary. It is just the same with the fantasy revolution of carnival, when the morning after the merriment the sun will rise on a thousand empty wine bottles, gnawed chicken legs and lost virginities and everyday life will resume, not without a certain ambiguous sense of relief. Or think of stage comedy, where the audience is never in any doubt that the order so delightfully disrupted will be restored, perhaps even reinforced by this fleeting attempt to flout it, and thus can blend its anarchic pleasures with a degree of conservative self-satisfaction. As in Ben Jonson's *The Alchemist*, Jane Austen's *Mansfield Park* or Dr Seuss's *The Cat in the Hat*, we can wreak some gloriously irresponsible havoc while the parental figure is absent, but would be devastated to learn that he or she might never return.

In the more innocuous kind of joke, so Freud argues, the humour springs from the release of the repressed impulse, while in obscene or abusive joking it stems from the relaxation of the repression itself. Blasphemous jokes also allow us to relax such inhibitions, as in the tale of the pope and Bill Clinton dying on the same day. By some bureaucratic blunder, Clinton was despatched to heaven while the pope was sent to hell. The error, however, was rapidly rectified, and the two men managed to snatch a quick word as they passed one another travelling in opposite directions – the pope remarking on how eager he was to see the Virgin Mary, and Clinton informing him that he was just ten minutes too late.

In Freud's view, the pleasurable form of the joke itself (wordplay, snatches of nonsense, absurd associations and so on) may lead the superego to relax its vigilance for a moment, which then allows the anarchic id an opportunity to thrust the censored feeling to the fore. The 'forepleasure' of the joke's verbal form, as Freud calls it, lowers our inhibitions, softens us up and in doing so cajoles us into accepting the joke's sexual or aggressive content, as we might not otherwise be ready to do. Laughing is in this sense a failure of repression; yet we are amused because we acknowledge the force of the inhibition in the very act of violating it, so that, as Sándor Ferenczi points out, a totally virtuous individual would laugh no more than a totally villainous one. The former would not harbour discreditable feelings in the first place, while the latter would not recognise the force of the prohibition and would therefore feel no particular thrill in transgressing it.[10] As Freud points out, we may be less moral than we like to think, but we are also more moral than we imagine. Like the neurotic symptom, jokes for the release theory are compromise formations, incorporating both the act of repression and the instinct being curbed.

So it is that the joke for Freud is a double-dealing rogue which serves two masters at once. It must bow to the authority of the superego while assiduously promoting the interests of the id. In the little insurrection of the wisecrack we can reap the pleasures of rebellion while simultaneously disavowing them, since it is, after all, only a joke. As Olivia remarks in *Twelfth Night*, there is no harm in an allowed Fool. On the contrary, the licensed jester who sends up social convention is a thoroughly conventional figure himself. Indeed, his irreverence may end up reinforcing social norms by demonstrating how remarkably resilient they are, how good-humouredly capable of surviving any amount of mockery. The most durable social order is the one secure enough not only to tolerate deviance but actively to encourage it.

A good deal of humour involves what Freud knows as desublimation. The energies we invest in some noble ideal or exalted alter ego are released as laughter when it is rudely punctured. Since sustaining such ideals involves a degree of psychological strain, not having to do so can be a gratifying sensation. We are now free from having to maintain a reputable moral front and can reap the delectable fruits of being openly crude, cynical, selfish, obtuse, insulting, morally indolent, emotionally anaesthetised and outrageously self-indulgent. But we can also be enjoyably released from the exigencies of sense-making itself, what Freud calls 'the compulsion of logic', a process that imposes unwelcome constraints on the unruly unconscious. Hence our delight in the surreal and absurd, in a world in which anything is possible, such as (in an episode of BBC

14

Radio's *The Goon Show*) the crafty device of floating a life-size cardboard replica of the British Isles off the British Isles in order to fool German bomber crews during the Second World War. The nineteenth-century philosopher Alexander Bain speaks of 'The posture of artificial and constrained seriousness demanded by the grave necessities of life',[11] restrictions of which a Victorian like himself was likely to be especially aware; and it is this solemn stance towards the world that humour allows us momentarily to shuck off. Everyday life involves sustaining a number of polite fictions: that we take a consuming interest in the health and well-being of our most casual acquaintances, that we never think about sex for a single moment, that we are thoroughly familiar with the later work of Schoenberg and so on. It is pleasant to drop the mask for a moment and strike up a comedic solidarity of weakness. Bain goes on to combine this release theory with a version of the superiority thesis, which we shall be investigating later. If we rejoice in seeing the high brought low, a deflation which allows us to relax a certain psychological tension, it is partly because we can now condescend to those by whom we were previously intimidated. We shall see later how a number of theorists combine different theories of humour in this way.

In the same spirit, Sándor Ferenczi remarks that 'remaining serious is a successful repression'.[12] Joking is thus a brief vacation from the mild oppressiveness of everyday meaning, which is itself a form of sublimation. The construction of social reality is a strenuous business which demands a sustained effort, and humour allows us to relax our mental muscles. It is as though beneath our more rational faculties there lies a darker, dishevelled, more cynical subtext which shadows our conventional social behaviour at every point, and which occasionally erupts into the open in the form of madness, criminality, erotic fantasy or an exuberant shaft of wit. It is a subtext which invades the daylight world on a large scale in such literary forms as Gothic fiction. One is reminded, too, of the Monty Python sketch in which a shopkeeper obsequiously serving a customer breaks suddenly into a torrent of foul abuse before reverting to his customary deferential self. On the other hand, there are forms of humour which are more instances of repression than resistances to it. Good, clean, hearty fun, for example. Boy Scout japes and general male joshing are anxious, aggressive ways of fending off subtleties of feeling and psychological complexities, all of which pose a threat to the world of mutual towel-slapping and beating drums while bare-chested deep in the woods.

What Bain perceives in his pre-Freudian way is that the maintenance of everyday reality itself demands of us a continuous repression. It is as though we are all really play-actors in our conventional social roles, sticking solemnly to our meticulously scripted parts but ready at the slightest fluff or stumble to dissolve into infantile, uproariously irresponsible laughter at the sheer arbitrariness and absurdity of the whole charade.

Meaning itself involves a degree of psychic strain, dependent as it is on excluding possibilities which swarm in from the unconscious. If excrement plays such a key role in comedy, it is partly because shit is the very model of meaninglessness, levelling all distinctions of sense and value to the same endlessly self-identical stuff. The line between comedy and cynicism can thus be alarmingly thin. Seeing everything as shit may represent a blessed emancipation from the rigours of hierarchy and the terrorism of high-minded ideals, but it is also unnervingly close to the concentration camp. If humour can deflate the pompous and pretentious in the name of some more viable conception of human dignity, it can also strike, Iago-like, at the very notion of value, which in turn depends on the possibility of meaning.

Take, for example, the story of the factory worker whose job it was to press a lever every few minutes. After many years at this task he discovered that the lever was not connected to anything, and suffered a severe breakdown as a result. One of the most disturbing aspects of this anecdote is that it is mildly funny. Released from the burden of meaning, we are amused by the absurdity of the situation at the same time as we are horrified by it. Futility is both alluring and appalling. Or take the tale of a group of patients in a psychiatric hospital who decided to commit collective suicide. Since there were no pills or weapons to hand, one of the group stood with his feet in a bucket of water and his finger in a light socket, while the others

17

clung on to him as one of them threw the switch. This, too, has its darkly entertaining aspect. We are dismayed by the misery that drove these men and women to such desperate extremes, while suppressing a wry smile at the ludicrousness of their situation. Death, wreathed as it is in portentous significance, is momentarily disarmed, reduced to Beckettian farce, so that the energy we invest in repressing the fact of our own mortality can be discharged in laughter. In both these cases, humour involves a brutal disregard for human value, a value that we nonetheless continue to cherish. We can dip into senselessness for a blessed moment without having to sign on for some of its more frightful consequences. If we are gratified by these strikes against the superego, however, it is partly because (though both of these incidents actually happened) we are in the presence of a piece of language rather than the real thing. At the same time, as Freud argues in an essay on humour, the superego may take pity on the ego and reinforce its narcissism. It may address it in consolatory tones, assuring it of its invulnerability by pointing out that there is no need for it to be anxious, since the world, after all, is just a joke.[13]

Bucking the tyranny of what Freud calls the reality principle, as jokes can be seen to do, affords us a certain infantile satisfaction, as we regress to a condition which pre-dates the jealously enforced divisions and precisions of the symbolic order and are able to throw logic, congruity and linearity to the winds. The failure of physical coordination induced by intense laughter is an outward sign of this reversion to primal helpless-ness. Humour does for adults what play does for children, namely liberates them from the despotism of the reality prin-ciple and allows the pleasure principle some scrupulously regu-lated free play. Infants and toddlers may not be accomplished wits or maestros of the well-timed gag, but they delight in the zany and nonsensical, as well as in the kind of babbling that might later become either poetry ('mouth music', as Seamus Heaney calls it) or surreal humour. They are, however, strangers to the kind of comedy that depends upon deviating from estab-lished norms, since they have as yet no grasp of them. You cannot defamiliarise a situation, and thus provoke a smile, when everything is still wondrously unfamiliar.

If carnival turns on a swoop from high to low, sexuality also manifests this bathetic movement from the sublime to the ridiculous, high-flying idealism to the workaday stuff of the senses. This is doubtless one reason why it is always a reli-able source of humour, along with the fact that repression in this province of human affairs is particularly robust, and the release of it correspondingly pleasurable. Since humour involves a gratifying release of tension which mimes the event of orgasm, even non-sexual varieties of it have subdued sexual overtones. Sexuality is a matter of physical desire but also of signs and values, and thus exists on the borderline between the somatic and semiotic. Pitched between romance and a romp, too much meaning and too little, it is an inherently ambiguous

19

phenomenon. Few human activities are at once so exotic yet so banally predictable. How can a few inches of flesh, or a few perfunctory thrusts of the loins, launch a thousand ships? How can the question of who copulates with whom, an observer from Alpha Centauri might ponder, constitute an issue for which men and women will howl, weep and kill?

Nothing is more central to traditional comedy than marriage, in which the somatic and semiotic are ideally at one, as the union of two bodies becomes the medium of a unity of souls. Yet comedies like Shakespeare's *A Midsummer Night's Dream* also alert us to the arbitrary status of these affinities, which could after all always have been different and perhaps a few scenes ago actually were. Body and spirit will not slot together quite so smoothly. If Puck in the *Dream* is too much restive spirit, the rude mechanicals are too much solid body. Something of the same might be said of the polarity between Ariel and Caliban in *The Tempest*. There is a fissure at the heart of humanity, which will not be easily healed by a happy ending. Nature and culture meet in sexuality, but their encounter is always an uneasy one. Perhaps it is for this reason that there is a wayward, unassimilable element at the close of some comedies, a surly Malvolio who refuses to join in the festivities, in order to remind us of the factitious, purely conventional nature of resolutions which might otherwise appear providential.

Matthew Bevis writes of the human creature as 'an animal which finds its own animality either objectionable or funny', and speaks wittily of 'the double act that we are'.[14] For Jonathan Swift, a certain grotesque or bathetic comedy is built into the contradictory amalgam of body and spirit we know as humanity. 'All men are necessarily comic,' comments Wyndham Lewis, 'for they are all *things*, or physical bodies, behaving as *persons*.'[15] 'What is funny, finally,' comments Simon Critchley, 'is the fact of having a body'[16] – more precisely, one might claim, the incongruity involved in neither quite having a body nor quite being one. We are, in short, comic creatures even before we have cracked a joke, and a good deal of humour exploits this fissure or self-division in our make-up. 'The aim of a joke,' remarks George Orwell, 'is not to degrade the human being, but to remind him that he is already degraded.'[17] When it comes to the linguistic animal, incongruity goes all the way down. Since we can objectify our own animality but not dissever ourselves from it, a certain irony is structural to the human species. To disown our animal existence altogether would be a form of madness, as Gulliver illustrates at the end of Swift's novel, but to be nothing but a body is to be a Yahoo. We are constituted in a way that allows us to reach beyond our own corporeal limits, a condition more commonly known as making history. As such, we belong to our own bodies in a way that permits us to put them at arm's length, which is not true of even the smartest of slugs.

Bathos – a too-sudden tumble from the exalted to the everyday – involves both release and incongruity; and incongruity, as we shall see later, lies at the heart of the currently most popular theory of how humour functions. To idealise involves a certain psychological effort, one which it is gratifying to relax and discharge in the form of laughter. Bathos, to be sure, is not the only way in which such psychic release can come about. For the so-called release theory, all humour involves this deflationary effect, as in a rush of desublimation we economise on the energy we invest in serious matters, or in the repression of certain illicit desires, and expend it instead in the form of laughter. Even so, the bathetic is especially marked in British comedy, not least because of the insistence of the class system. Legendary British comedians such as Tony Hancock, Frankie Howerd and Kenneth Williams all trade on sudden, indecorous shifts from the civilised tones of the cultivated middle classes to the blunter idiom of the populace. It is as if such comics contain contending social classes within their own person, and as such figure as a kind of walking class struggle. Taking poshness down a peg or two is a familiar British pastime, one that combines the nation's satirical impulse with its penchant for self-deprecation. English humour often revolves on a conflict of class cultures. One calls to mind Monty Python's 'Summarise Proust' contest, a popular television game in which competitors each have two minutes to summarise the plot of Proust's three-thousand-odd-page novel, first in evening dress and then in a bathing costume.

For quite different social reasons, bathos is also a key device in Irish humour. A society with a rich legacy of ancient art, monastic learning and scholastic thought is likely to be peculiarly conscious of the gap between this erudite culture and the conditions of everyday life in a wretchedly backward colony. So it is that the final book of the Anglo-Irish Jonathan Swift's *Gulliver's Travels* veers between the absurdly high-minded Houyhnhnms and the bestial, shit-coated Yahoos, allowing the reader no normative middle ground on which to stand. In his *Thoughts on Laughter*, the eighteenth-century Ulster philosopher Francis Hutcheson maintains that a good deal of humour arises from an incongruous coupling of grandeur and profanity, or dignity and meanness, which he extols as the very spirit of burlesque. One takes it he has comic parody, not striptease, in mind. Laurence Sterne's *Tristram Shandy* counterpoints the pathologically rationalist Walter Shandy, who is pure mind, with his son Tristram, who is all body. W. B. Yeats pitches Crazy Jane against the Bishop, the carnivalesque vitality of the peasant against a stifling orthodox spirituality. James Joyce's *Ulysses* splits down the middle between the esoteric meditations of Stephen Dedalus and the mundane reflections of Leopold Bloom.

In Samuel Beckett's *Waiting for Godot*, a venerable scholastic tradition is splintering before our eyes, reduced in Pozzo's garbled speech to a heap of fragments. Flann O'Brien's fiction plays off abstruse metaphysical speculation against the threadbare platitudes of pub talk. In Ireland today, one has only to use the phrase 'the *Skibbereen Eagle*' to evoke a sense of bathos. Skibbereen is an unremarkable town in County Cork whose newspaper, the *Eagle*, solemnly assured its readers in an editorial at the end of the First World War that it was 'keeping a close eye on the Treaty of Versailles'. Small nations with a history of hardship tend to be especially amused by those among their own ranks who get above themselves.

There is, however, a deeper meaning of bathos. Writing of the critic William Empson, Christopher Norris argues that the key terms he investigates in his *The Structure of Complex Words* ('fool', 'dog', 'honest' and so on) play their part in generating 'a down-to-earth quality of healthy scepticism which ... permits their users to build up a trust in human nature on a shared knowledge of its needs and attendant weaknesses'.[18] It is, in effect, a description of the comic spirit. But it is also an account of what Empson elsewhere calls pastoral, a way of seeing which views the complex and sophisticated as embedded in the commonplace. Pastoral in his view signifies among other things a large-minded plebeian wisdom which knows when not to ask too much of others. You must love and admire the 'high' human values of truth, beauty, courage and the like; but you must not be excessively dejected if men and women fail to live up to these sublime ideals, or terrorise them with such notions in a way which makes their weaknesses painful to them. As such, the pastoral sensibility has something in common with Antonio Gramsci's 'good sense', the routine practical wisdom of those who, more conversant with the material world than their superiors, are less likely to be bamboozled by florid flights of rhetoric. 'The most refined desires,' Empson comments in both pastoral and Freudian vein, 'are inherent in the plainest, and would be false if they weren't.'[19] Some individuals, he acknowledges, are more subtle and delicate than others, and this need not matter – indeed, it may be a positive enrichment, provided such distinctions do not wreak social damage. But the most seductive subtleties, the most dazzling displays of heroism, virtue and intellect, are a poor thing compared to our common humanity, and whenever we are forced to choose it is always better to choose the latter. It is thus that bathos ceases to be a mere comic trope and becomes instead a moral and political vision.

In *The Book of Laughter and Forgetting*, the Czech novelist Milan Kundera contrasts what he calls angelic and demonic views of human existence. The angelic sees the world as orderly, harmonious and stuffed to the seams with meaning. In the kingdom of the angels, everything is instantly, oppressively meaningful, and no shadow of ambiguity can be tolerated. The whole of reality is drearily legible and intelligible. As for those in the grip of paranoia, there is no room for the random or contingent. Whatever happens happens by necessity, as part of some grand narrative in which every feature of existence has its allotted function. Nothing is negative, awry, deficient or dysfunctional; instead, in this anodyne angelic vision, humankind marches beaming towards the future, shouting, 'Long Live Life!' There is a civilised mode of laughter associated with this way of seeing – a rejoicing over how shapely, meaningful and wisely conceived the world is. Among other things, it is the world of Soviet dogma in which Kundera spent the early decades of his life, though it also bears a marked resemblance to contemporary American ideology, with its compulsively upbeat, you-can-be-anything-you-want version of reality. In this euphoric realm, there are no catastrophes, simply challenges. The speech to which it gives rise is what Kundera calls 'shitless', whereas the demonic is full of shit. As we have seen already, it revels in the vision of a world purged of meaning and value, one in which everything is excrementally indistinguishable from everything else. If the angelic suffers from an excess of meaning, the demonic is afflicted by a lack of it.

Even so, the demonic has its uses. Its role in social existence is to disrupt the anodyne certainties of the angelic by figuring as the grit in its oyster, the glitch in its mechanism, the perverse, refractory factor in any social order. As such, it has a certain affinity with the Lacanian Real. The demonic is the cackle of mocking laughter which deflates the pretensions of the angelic, puncturing its portentousness. It is, as the Devil himself comments in Dostoevsky's *The Brothers Karamazov*, the wayward, cross-grained element which prevents the world from collapsing on itself under the weight of its own suffocating blandness. His own role, he tells Ivan Karamazov, is to act as a form of friction or negativity within God's Creation, one which will prevent it from withering away from sheer boredom. Without him, the world would be 'nothing but Hosannas'. If this deviant factor were to be expunged, cosmic order would break out and put an end to everything. Devils are natural deconstructionists.

Humour of this kind is the amusement that springs from things being out of order, estranged or defamiliarised, deprived for a moment of their allotted role in the overall scheme of things. We laugh when some phenomenon seems suddenly out of place, when things go off the rails or are thrown out of kilter. Such comedy represents a momentary respite from the tyrannical legibility of the world, a realm of lost innocence which pre-dates our calamitous fall into meaning. It disturbs the equipoise of the universe, as in the joke or spontaneous shaft of wit, or bleaches it of coherent meaning altogether, as with the goonish, fantastic, preposterous and surreal. The literally meaningless sound of laughter enacts this haemorrhage of sense. It is not surprising, then, that the demonic is so often associated with humour – that hell traditionally resounds with the obscene cackling, sniggering and guffawing of those lost souls who believe they have seen through human value and exposed it as the pompous fraud that it is. Thomas Mann speaks of this laughter in *Doctor Faustus* as 'a luciferian sardonic mood', a 'hellish merriment' of 'yelling, screeching, bawling, bleating, howling, piping . . . the mocking, exultant laughter of the Pit'.[20] The demonic versus the angelic is Iago against Othello, or Milton's smouldering Satan against his constipated bureaucrat of a Deity. 'Laughter is Satanic,' writes Charles Baudelaire; 'it is therefore profoundly human.'[21] The devils cannot suppress a spasm of incredulous laughter at the sheer gullibility of men and women, their pathetic eagerness to believe that their gratuitous, paper-thin meanings and values are as solid as flatirons.

In an innovative study of comedy, Alenka Zupančič sees jokes as microcosms of 'the paradoxical and contingent constitution of our world'.[22] What they do is raise to consciousness the chancy, ungrounded nature of our sense-making. They are, so to speak, the hidden truth of the symbolic order of language, with its rational, apparently natural version of reality. The signifiers that constitute that order are in fact arbitrary marks and sounds; and if they are to function effectively, they must be flexible, ambiguous and free-floating enough to be combined in a variety of different ways, including absurd and outrageous ones. What makes for sense, then, must also logically make for nonsense. Each is an indispensable condition of the other. Zupančič speaks of 'universal nonsense as the presupposition of all sense'.[23] For Freud too, it is non-meaning that lies at the root of meaning. 'The value of the joke,' writes Jacques Lacan, '. . . is its possibility to play on the fundamental non-sense of all usages of sense.'[24] Jokes let the contingently constructed nature of social reality out of the bag, and hence betray its fragility. 'On a certain level,' Zupančič comments, 'there is a dimension of precariousness and fundamental uncertainty in our very world that gets articulated or becomes manifest in every joke.'[25] One might say the same of the symbolic order seen as an orderly structure of kinship roles, governed by a set of rules for their appropriate combination. It is in the nature of such an order that if it is to function properly, it must also be capable of functioning improperly. If the laws that regulate it can give rise to legitimate permutations of roles, they can also generate illicit ones. Incest, for example.

This instability of social meaning is likely to be most obvious to an outsider. So it is that from Congreve, Farquhar, Steele, Macklin and Goldsmith to Sheridan, Wilde, Shaw and Behan, English stage comedy has been dominated by a lineage of Irish émigrés, writers who washed up in the English metropolis with little but their wits to hawk and proceeded to turn their hybrid status as insider/outsiders to fruitful dramatic use. As English speakers themselves, a number of them in fact of Anglo-Irish descent, they were sufficiently conversant with mainland conventions to master them successfully, while sufficiently estranged from them to have a quick satirical eye for their absurdities. Assumptions that might seem self-evident to the British could strike them as flagrantly factitious, and comic art could be plucked from this discrepancy. A conflict between nature and artifice is a staple comic motif, and few were better placed to feel it on their pulses than those Irish authors who frequented the English clubs and coffee houses without ever quite feeling that they were much more than house guests of the London literati.

What comedy exists to disrupt, then, is cosmos, in the sense of the world viewed as a rational, virtuous, beautiful, well-ordered whole. That this is so is in one sense ironic, since a phrase like *The Divine Comedy* signifies just such a vision.[26] Comedy in this metaphysical sense of the term, as we shall see later, reflects the quasi-mystical assurance that, despite appearances to the contrary, all is fundamentally well with humanity. The New Testament is a comic document in just this sense, though it is aware that the price of such faith is fearfully steep. It is nothing less than death and self-dispossession. Stage comedy preserves a sense of order and design at the level of form, while questioning this symmetry in its disruptive content. It is as if the form is utopian or angelic, while the content is satiric or demonic. In the end, a piece of comedy tends to shift from the latter state to the former. The action may revolve on a crisis in the symbolic order, but its ultimate aim is to repair, restore and reconcile. It is thus that comedy as crisis gives way to comedy as cosmos. The angelic supervenes on the demonic, though not without a struggle.

We may turn finally to the greatest of all modern philosophers of comedy, the Russian scholar Mikhail Bakhtin, whose path-breaking work on the subject, *Rabelais and his World*, was written in the depths of the Stalinist era. Indeed, it was intended among other things as a coded critique of that regime, a dissidence that was eventually to drive the author into exile. Laughter in Bakhtin's eyes is not only a response to comic events but a distinctive form of knowledge. It 'has a deep philosophical meaning', he writes,

> it is one of the essential forms of the truth concerning the world as a whole, concerning history and man; it is a peculiar point of view relative to the world; the world is seen anew, no less (and perhaps more) profoundly than when seen from the serious standpoint. Therefore, laughter is just as admissible in great literature, posing universal problems, as seriousness. Certain essential aspects of the world are accessible only to laughter.[27]

Like an effective work of art, comedy lights up the world from a distinctive angle, and does so in a way no other social practice can.

The genre of comic art Bakhtin has in mind is carnivalesque humour, which we shall be examining in more detail later. Carnival in his eyes is not only a form of popular festivity but an entire world view, of which carnivalesque laughter is, so to speak, the articulate language. It is a tongue that in Bakhtin's terms is both philosophical and universal. In post-Renaissance Europe, so he claims, the essential truth of the world and humanity can no longer be expressed in this joyful idiom, given over as it is to 'serious' doctrinal discourse. It had also been eliminated from the formal cult and ideology of the medieval era, taking up home instead in the informal subculture of carnival. 'The serious aspects of class culture,' Bakhtin writes, 'are official and authoritarian; they are combined with violence, prohibitions, limitations and always contain an element of fear and of intimidation. These elements prevailed in the Middle Ages. Laughter, on the contrary, overcomes fear, for it knows no inhibitions, no limitations. Its idiom is never used by violence and authority.'[28]

In this wide-eyed idealising of popular diversions, Bakhtin seems to have forgotten about the traditional function of bread and circuses. He is also of course blissfully ignorant of TV game shows or right-wing comedians. Carnivalesque laughter, he rhapsodises, is 'the defeat of divine and human power, of authoritarian commandments and prohibitions, of death and punishment after death, hell and all that is more terrifying than the earth itself . . . The acute awareness of victory over fear is an essential element of medieval laughter . . . All that was terrifying becomes grotesque.'[29] Such comedy, political to its core, signals 'the defeat of power, of earthly kings, of the earthly upper classes, of all that oppresses and restricts'.[30] It is linked with 'the procreating act, with birth, renewal, fertility, abundance'.[31] 'For the medieval parodist', Bakhtin observes in rashly hyperbolic style, everything without exception was comic. Laughter was as universal as seriousness; it was directed at the whole world, at history, at all societies, at ideology. It was the world's second truth extended to everything and from which nothing is taken away. It was, as it were, the festive aspect of the whole world in all its elements, the second revelation of the world in play and laughter.[32]

The comic and the serious are clashing modes of cognition, competing versions of the nature of reality, not just alternative moods or discursive modes.

Since carnival is a strictly episodic affair, the victories of which Bakhtin speaks with such gusto are in fact somewhat flimsy. Even so, what is intriguing about his theory of laughter is that it treats carnival, apparently the most fantastical of affairs, as the ultimate form of realism, and this both ethically and epistemologically. What yields us the truth of reality is an extravaganza. As a privileged form of cognition, carnivalesque laughter grasps the world as it actually is, in its ceaseless growth, decay, fertility, mutability, rebirth and renewal, and in doing so undercuts the spuriously eternal schemas of official ideology. Only laughter can yield us the inner substance of reality. It must, Bakhtin insists, 'liberate the gay truth of the world from the veils of gloomy lies spun by the seriousness of fear, suffering, and violence'.[33] The Victorian novelist George Meredith speaks rather similarly of comedy as the medicine 'for the poison of delusion'.[34] Because such humour is bound up for Bakhtin with the event of carnival, it is a practical rather than contemplative mode of cognition. Only the rumbustious carnivalesque spirit, joyful, fearless and free, is audacious enough to affirm reality in all its volatile, provisional, unfinished, unstable, open-ended character, and thus to dispense with stout foundations, metaphysical guarantees and transcendental signifiers. The 'sober optimism' of the comic outlook is the world demystified, purged of ideological illusion, unmasked as temporal, material and mercurial to its roots.

Why change and instability should be thought precious in themselves, given that they can sometimes prove catastrophic, remains unclear. For Bakhtin, they are simply immanent features of reality, which any realist epistemology must recognise as such – though why what is true from an epistemological viewpoint should also be acceptable from an ethical one is left unargued. Plenty of thinkers have argued that we should act against the grain of reality, not conspire with it. Even so, the link between comedy and realism is a suggestive one. Humour may allow us to relax our drive to master and possess, and thus to see the object free from the compulsions of appetite and need. It no longer has meaning and value simply as part of some project of our own. Indeed, the laughing body is incapable of such agency. Comedy, like mechanical reproduction for Walter Benjamin, dispels the intimidatory aura of things, and in doing so brings them closer; but it also banishes any deep affect, and in that sense pushes them off to the point where we can grasp them without reference to our own clamorous demands and desires. In this absolution from immediate practice, humour has something in common with art.

We shall see later that Bakhtinian carnival can be violent and vituperative, but that this abrasiveness is caught up in a general spirit of affirmation and well-being. In the meantime, however, we may turn to a theory of humour of which this is far from the case.

2

SCOFFERS AND MOCKERS

If bathos describes a trajectory from high to low, so in a different sense does the so-called superiority theory of humour. The argument – that humour springs from a gratifying sense of the frailty, obtuseness or absurdity of one's fellow beings – is an ancient one. It can be found as early as the Book of Solomon, where Yahweh laughs at the calamities he has in store for the wicked. It is one of only a handful of instances of divine risibility in the Hebrew scriptures, most of which are scornful rather than affable. There is also an Augustinian tradition for which God laughs mockingly at the sinners in hell.[1] Barry Sanders notes that the first laugh in Western literature occurs in Book 1 of the *Iliad*, when the gods mock the limping gait of Hephaistos, god of fire.[2] Plato writes in the *Philebus* of comedy as arising from malicious mockery. Aristotle also treats humour as mostly abusive, though he allows for an innocuous brand of it as well, and with impeccable political correctness forbids laughing at others' misfortunes.[3]

Cicero points out in his 'On the Orator' that we laugh at human deformity, while Francis Bacon also sees the ludicrous and disfigured as sources of merriment. 'Some must cry,' reflects the narrator of Jean Rhys's novel *Good Morning, Midnight*, 'so that the others may be able to laugh the more heartily.' On this jaundiced view, the primary wellspring of humour is that joy in the miseries of others which the Germans call *Schadenfreude*. We scoff at delusions, self-deceptions, inflated self-importance, undisguised lechery, voracious egoism and lame self-rationalisation, as well as at the maladroit, cack-handed and boneheaded. In doing so, the ego can enjoy a certain illusory invulnerability. It can also gain a release of tension by trivialising the physical or moral misshapenness that causes it anxiety, satirically diminishing what discomfits it and cutting the fearful or distressing down to size. We might note, too, that when it comes to affairs of the mind, to be laughed at means having your case undercut rather than seriously contested, discounted rather than refuted, and is thus a particularly painful kind of humiliation.

The *locus classicus* of the superiority theory is to be found in Thomas Hobbes's celebrated comment in *Leviathan* that 'sudden glory is the passion that maketh those grimaces called laughter; and is caused either by some sudden act of their

own, that pleaseth them; or by the apprehension of some
deformed thing in another, by comparison whereof they
suddenly applaud themselves'.[4] We laugh because we become
aware of some 'eminency' in ourselves which contrasts either
with the infirmity of others, or with some previous failing of
our own. There is no conception here of humour as genial,
playful, affirmative or just delightfully nonsensical. A faculty
generally thought to represent some of the most engaging
features of humanity becomes an expression of some of the
least savoury. Even so, Hobbes goes on to insist that an excessive taste for other people's afflictions is a sign of pusillanimity,
and so is to be shunned. Great minds strive not to mock
others, and compare themselves only with the most able. He
touches here on one of the paradoxes of the superiority theory,
namely that those who jeer at others as inferior simply demon-
strate their own moral shabbiness. Joseph Addison endorses
the Hobbesian view in his journal *The Spectator*, writing of
humour as 'a secret elation and pride of heart', though he
acknowledges that there are cases where the assumption of
superiority may well be unwarranted.[5] Hegel argues in the
Philosophy of Fine Art that laughter springs from the self-
satisfaction involved in observing human aberrations. Charles
Darwin likewise sees humour as involving superiority, though
he also believes that incongruities play a part in it. A later
thinker couples the superiority thesis with the release theory
by claiming that breaking through social conventions yields

us a pleasurable sense of superiority to them, shedding our timorous conformism.[6] The Earl of Shaftesbury, by contrast, is spurred by his neo-Platonic sense of cosmic and social harmony to claim that only those 'of slavish principles ... affect a superiority over the vulgar, and despise the multitude'.[7]

As an account of humour as a whole, the superiority theory is vastly implausible, though it has had some recent defenders.[8] Indeed, it is not only implausible but actually rather funny. There is something amusingly perverse in insisting that what seem on the face of it high spirits, tokens of comradeship or innocent entertainment are always and everywhere motivated by a malign urge to do others down. What looks like affability is supposedly powered by spite, malice, arrogance and aggression. 'Any form of humour,' observes the poet Robert Frost, 'shows fear and inferiority. Irony is simply a kind of guardedness ... At bottom the world isn't a joke. We only joke about it to avoid an issue with someone ... Humour is the most engaging cowardice.'[9] Even in the case of derisive humour, however, the sense of superiority may be strictly qualified. We may chuckle at someone whose trousers fall down while regarding them as superior to ourselves in everything but their choice of belts. In any case, having your trousers fall down is not a moral shortcoming. For one's legs to be suddenly exposed to public view does not betoken some ontologically inferior status. We can also feel smug about someone's infirmity while being aware that we share it ourselves. You can snigger at the short-sighted while being myopic yourself. Elvis Presley, a drug addict, was a zealous opponent of drugs. Besides, even if all humour involves rating something as inferior, not all inferiority is a question of humour. We do not thrash helplessly on the floor because babies cannot grasp the principles of set theory or snakes find it hard to operate dishwashers.

The Earl of Shaftesbury, despite his scepticism of the Hobbesian view, splices a version of humour as malicious with the release theory, an uncommon combination of cases. When the natural spirits of men and women are released from constraint, then 'whether it be burlesque, mimicry or buffoonery, they will be glad at any rate to vent themselves, and be revenged on their constrainers'.[10] In his treatise on laughter, not the most familiar of literary genres in Protestant Ulster, the philosopher Francis Hutcheson has great fun in demolishing Hobbes's unappetising notions. 'It is a great pity,' he writes sardonically, 'that we had not an infirmary or lazar-house to retire to in the cloudy weather, to get an afternoon of laughter at these inferior objects . . .'[11] It is also curious, he adds with faux bemusement, that the Hobbesians do not assiduously collect inferior creatures like owls, snails and oysters 'to be merry upon'. In 'The Laugh of the Medusa', Hélène Cixous sees women's laughter as a puncturing of male pretentions, and thus as a strike at superiority rather than a specimen of it.[12] Comedy may be less an exercise in power than a contestation of it. It can be a field of symbolic struggle, not simply the sneering of the powerful.

Henri Bergson's notion of humour as a response to a certain inelasticity in social existence is a species of superiority theory. All humour, Bergson maintains, is really intended to humiliate, involving as it does a form of secret Freemasonry or complicity with those who share one's contemptuous view. On this theory, we laugh at people and things that become mindlessly automated, obsessive, stuck in a groove, unable to adapt themselves to their circumstances. The eccentric, who is stuck in the groove of himself, is one such example, and the point of humour is to whip these aberrations back into line by the power of ridicule. Laughter thus acts as a social corrective, restraining social deviancy, tempering rigidities of character and behaviour and thus producing the psychological plasticity that modern societies demand. Comedy, then, has direct social utility, as it does for a rich heritage of social satire from Juvenal to Evelyn Waugh. We think of humour as gratuitous and nonfunctional, but this is far from so. On the contrary, one of its most traditional functions has been social reform. If men and women cannot be scolded into virtue, they might always be satirised into it. Antagonism is thus harnessed to civilised ends. 'Men have been laughed out of faults which a sermon could not reform,' writes Francis Hutcheson.[13] This, to be sure, is not the only use of humour. It can also be deployed to manipulate or cajole, ingratiate or disarm, break the ice, seal a

41

contract, soothe or inflict an injury. As far as the latter goes, one should note that the word 'sarcasm' comes from an ancient Greek term meaning to tear the flesh. Humour can be a question of defence or affirmation, subversion or celebration, solidarity or critique. It is not just a vacation from such utilitarian matters.

Think, for example, of the novels of Henry Fielding, who like most English novelists before Thomas Hardy (though with the striking exception of his contemporary Samuel Richardson) is a comic writer. It is comedy that will act as an agent of social improvement by repairing misfortune, resolving conflicts, scourging vice and rewarding virtue. By whipping excessive aberrations back into line, it can restore a degree of order and equipoise to a society pitched temporarily into disarray. Jane Austen's novels are hardly side-splitting, but they, too, are comic in just this sense. Perhaps there is a decidedly uncomic implication that such justice can now only ever be poetic – that fiction alone is the place where social conflicts can be massaged and contradictions reconciled. Comic art of this kind presents us with a fantasy of social harmony, and is thus utopian and ideological at the same time.

Comedy for Bergson is a matter of intelligence, not feeling. It demands what he calls, in a felicitous phrase, 'a momentary anaesthesia of the heart'.[14] Freud, too, sees it as incompatible with any strong affect. In fact, it allows us to economise on such affects, converting our pity or compassion into jesting.

On the superiority theory, then, humour is essentially heart-less. Empathy is its deadly enemy. Sentimentalism, observes André Breton in his anthology *Black Humour*, is the mortal foe of humour. Another theorist speculates that laughter evolved as an antidote to sympathy, shielding us from the sufferings of others.[15] Grimly resolved to stretch the superi-ority thesis to cover every conceivable form of humour, F. H. Buckley even manages to rope in carnival, which he sees as flaunting the vitality of the pleasure-loving masses over their emotionally anaemic rulers.[16] The novelist Angela Carter describes comedy as tragedy that happens to other people, while Mel Brooks remarks that tragedy is when one cuts one's finger, and comedy is when someone else walks into an open sewer and dies. On this view, to laugh is to be engaged with reality, since you must have a vivid sense of what you find amusing, but at the same time to be distanced, aloof, dismis-sive, belittling. Observing the gaffes and bloomers of others, we can reap a spurious sense of invulnerability, one which may in turn yield a bogus feeling of immortality. By projecting its own deficiencies on to others, the poor, pitiable ego can feel for a blessed moment beyond harm, as it can in the state that the eighteenth century knew as the sublime. By dint of such defence mechanisms, it can save itself an overload of distress and anxiety.

It is their blank, uninflected, scrupulously deadpan style ('His sentence of seven years' penal servitude was rather a blow') that forestalls a surplus of psychological distress in the early satirical novels of Evelyn Waugh, as the most grotesque of characters and improbable of events are filtered through a neutral style which flattens them to two dimensions, purges them of affect and drains them of interiority. This is an exercise in satirical superiority at the expense of the debutantes, upper-class drones and purple-faced clubmen who populate Waugh's fiction, but it is also a devious way of avoiding having to pass judgement on them. The moral and emotional anaesthesia of the characters themselves – their inability to belong to their own experience – is reflected in the novels' own meticulously externalised treatment of them, so that no genuine criticism of this morally vacuous world can be articulated, either by the narrator or by its victims and scapegoats. In this sense, the form of the novels makes them both superior to and complicit with their subject matter. Their mode of perception, dispassionate though it may appear, connives in the behaviour it surveys. Meanwhile the reader, relieved of the strain of having to decipher nuances of feeling and complexities of character, can relax and laugh all the louder.

Comedy can be a demeaning term as well as an affirmative one. To call someone a comedian, unless that is their line of work, is not the most fulsome of compliments. The comedian Ken Dodd was successfully defended against a charge of tax evasion by a barrister who argued that though some accountants were comedians, not many comedians were accountants. The phrase 'the human comedy' may suggest a robust delight in the dynamism and diversity of human existence, as with Balzac's *Human Comedy*; but it can also imply that the human species is something of a joke, not to be taken too seriously. Indeed, to contemplate it from a seat in the gods, so to speak, may give rise to a sense of squalid farce, as it does with that gloomiest of philosophers, Arthur Schopenhauer. For all his lugubrious cast of mind, Schopenhauer finds it impossible to suppress a snort of incredulous laughter at the sight of these pathetic insects known as human beings – what he calls 'this world of constantly needy creatures who continue for a time merely by devouring one another, pass their existence in anxiety and want, and often endure terrible afflictions, until they fall at last into the arms of death'. There is no grand goal to this 'battle-ground of tormented and agonised beings', only 'momentary gratification, fleeting pleasure conditioned by wants, much and long suffering, constant struggle, *bellum omnium*, everything a hunter and everything hunted, pressure, want, need and anxiety, shrieking and howling; and this goes on *in saecula saeculorum* or until once again the crust of the planet breaks'.[17]

For all its disgust, there is something darkly comic about this vision. The comedy lies in the incongruity between how things look from this Olympian standpoint and the zeal with which men and women pursue their various futile projects, utterly convinced of their own supreme importance. It is a double optic one also finds in the fiction of Thomas Hardy, a novelist who will first park his camera, so to speak, behind a character's shoulder, then pull it back and broaden the shot to show him or her as a tiny speck crawling across a vast natural landscape. Comedy in this sense, as with the satire of Swift, involves a gesture of savage diminishment, one which treads a thin line between the nihilistic and the therapeutic. Human diversity is reduced from this height to a few stock types, each convinced of his or her freedom and uniqueness while acting in blind accordance with an iron destiny known as character. As with all farce, it is a way of seeing that combines the comic with the meaningless.

Yet detachment can also breed a kind of compassion. To reflect that nothing matters much may allow us to relax, and sympathy for others can flow from this easing of tension. We can adopt a more ironic view of our own affairs, which no longer appear quite so pressing, and thus feel freer to respond to the (equally flimsy) affairs of others. Or one may turn one's eyes from their individual vices and attend instead to their general plight, in which case one's sympathy for their situation trades on a devaluing of their particularity. If one can look down on the human scene with a sense of nausea, one can also do so with a touch of sardonic amusement, as at the end of William Thackeray's *Vanity Fair*: 'Ah, *Vanitas Vanitatum!* Which of us is happy in this world? Which of us has his desire?

or, having it, is satisfied? – Come, children, let us shut up the box and the puppets, for our play is played out.' Characters we have known as flesh and blood creatures in the course of the novel are reduced in this final, wearily patronising gesture to painted dolls, as the whole complex action of the book becomes no more than an idle show to entertain a child.

Speaking of her own unremarkable lower-middle-class characters, George Eliot adopts a similar tone in *Adam Bede*:

These fellow-mortals, every one, must be accepted as they are: you can neither straighten their noses, nor brighten their wit, nor rectify their dispositions; and it is these people – amongst whom your life is passed – that it is needful you should tolerate, pity, and love: it is these more or less ugly, stupid, inconsistent people, whose movements of goodness you should be able to admire – for whom you should cherish all possible hopes, all possible patience . . . I find a source of delicious sympathy in these faithful pictures of a monotonous homely existence, which has been the fate of so many more among my fellow-mortals than a life of pomp or of absolute indigence, of tragic suffering or of world-stirring actions (Chapter 17).

Seen from this affectionately condescending distance, men and women are lacklustre, thick-headed and faintly repugnant; but they are not without value, however short they may fall of tragic heroism or visionary idealism. Along with this sense of ironic patronage goes a certain warm-hearted liberal sympathy for these droll creatures, as well as a wry tolerance of their quirks and foibles. Indeed, one's sympathy is worth all the more precisely because they are so hard to love. These pedestrian types are basically fairly hopeless, but this is not to say that they are malign. The mediocrity that makes their lives so drab also absolves them from any spectacular vices. If they were more heroic or resplendent, one might feel for them less. As long as one does not expect too much of such individuals (with the utopianists and revolutionaries in mind, Eliot goes on to upbraid 'lofty theories which only fit a world of extremes'), they are candidates for one's compassion, as well as being fit meat for one's entertainment. It is, however, a broad-mindedness that may bring in its wake some ominous political consequences: if men and women really are as flawed as this, they may require the smack of firm government.

On this gently demeaning estimate, human beings are not to be redeemed or revolutionised. They can only be what they are. Like actors in a play or characters in a novel, they can do no more than perform their meticulously scripted roles. From one's own superior vantage point, one can see just how conditioned their behaviour is, as though one were observing a nest of ants. They are not free and self-determining, even though they may need to assume they are so that social existence does not start to unravel. In W. B. Yeats's poem 'Easter 1916', John

MacBride is said to have 'resigned his part / In the casual comedy', but he can step outside that part only to die. It is possible to reap a certain melancholic pleasure from this bleak determinism. People may be undistinguished, but at least they are predictable. They will never do anything extraordinary, but you know where you are with them.

If human beings are seen as caught up in a set of pointless cycles, then this may inspire neither cynicism nor condescension but comedy. We can rest assured that nothing in these great whirlings and spirallings can ever truly be lost; that everything will eventually be restored with a slight difference; that every phenomenon is simply a fleeting combination of eternally abiding elements; and that if we ourselves are not immortal, then at least this can be said of the world spirit or mighty flow of matter of which we are part. So it is that Joyce's *Finnegans Wake*, unlike T. S. Eliot's *The Waste Land*, is able to rejoice in carnivalesque style in this vision of eternal return, while Joyce's compatriot W. B. Yeats looks to some future turn of the historical wheel which will restore the indomitable Anglo-Irishry to their place of privilege. The Chinamen in his poem 'Lapis Lazuli' gaze down from a lofty height on a varied scene of decay, destruction, violence and renewal, but the eyes with which they do so are gay.

There is cruelty and pain, then, but the world is to be affirmed in full knowledge of these facts. There is nothing new under the sun, and the fact that we have seen it all before saves us the psychological discomfort of coping with the unfamiliar. Because nothing in this stupendous work of art known as the cosmos can be altered, one must accept that human judgements are idle, that everything has its apportioned place, and that the only attitude one can adopt to the world is an aesthetic one. There is certainly no possibility of intervening to change it. Comedy and fatalism are thus in collusion. Relieved of the burden of moral conscience, we can gaze upon the cosmos knowing ourselves to be bound up with its imperishable stuff, even if it has no more regard for us than a wave of the ocean. This sense of deep-seated ease, of being at home in the universe, is one of the most profoundly comic of experiences. It is not, to be sure, comic in the sense of funny, but humour can flow from the equanimity it fosters. Nor, needless to say, is it beyond criticism. The profound is not necessarily the valid. This way of seeing can make nothing of the absolute loss on which the experience of tragedy turns. If everything is recycled and recuperated, there can be no irretrievable damage. It may also be a recipe for moral and political inertia. The most we can do is contemplate reality like some mighty work of art, knowing that we are as immune from coming to grief as Nature itself, serenely detached from the misfortunes that beset us on every side.

A sociologist of my acquaintance once entered his university department to find his secretary in tears. Having tried to console her, he wandered down the corridor and glanced into another office, where he saw another secretary in tears. 'One secretary in tears is a tragedy,' he told me, 'two is sociology.' Or, one might say, comedy, in the sense of the term just sketched. Sociologists are not concerned with individual phenomena, and neither is a good deal of comedy. It is the general design of human affairs as seen from some way off, with its shared modes of behaviour and ritually recurrent features, that seizes its attention. No form of art depends more deeply on a concept of human nature. High tragedy is exceptional, whereas comedy is commonplace. A second secretary weeping seems to devalue the grief of the first, shifting the focus from the individual to the overall pattern, distancing the first tearful secretary and thinning out our emotional response. There is, as we shall see later, something comic about such reflections and repetitions, which unbind the energy involved in attending to a single phenomenon. It is the doubling we find funny, not the distress. We expect things to differ from each other, so that to stumble across an unexpected case of identity is incongruous and therefore amusing. It is the only case in which incongruity is not a question of the clash of two or more different realities.

This eye to the overall design, along with a certain detachment from individual destinies, can be found in a great deal of stage comedy. Such drama draws us in, but it also typically fends us off, and does so for the most part by virtue of its form. One thinks of such magnificent theatre pieces as Ben

Jonson's *The Alchemist* or Oscar Wilde's *The Importance of Being Earnest*, which by stylising and formalising their actions, as well as by stereotyping their characters and foregrounding their language, hold us resolutely at arm's length even as we dissolve in delighted laughter. Faced with a comic stereotype, we can conserve the energy we would need to invest in savouring the intricacies of a realistic character, and so can discharge it in a chuckle or a snigger. Empathy would deal a fatal blow to such entertainment. This stylisation reaches its highpoint in farce, with its doublings, mirrorings, mismatchings, reversals, backfirings and substitutions, its crossovers, inversions, repetitions, double effects and outrageous coincidences, all of which formal symmetry represents a negative image of order. Characters are reduced to mere bearers of the action, emptied of their subjectivity to become so many cogs in a well-oiled machine. We would no sooner think of empathising with them than we would with a canary. In less farcical types of comedy, the plot may equally be thrust into prominence because it needs to function as a secular version of Providence. Virtuous characters cannot be shown to be working for their own advancement without souring our mirth a little, in which case the narrative itself must assume the task of endowing them with a landed estate, a long-lost sibling or a suitably well-heeled marriage partner, at some inevitable cost to realist credibility. What are the odds against a real-life Oliver Twist ending up in muslin shirt and velvet jacket? Since a realist portrayal of a wicked world is likely to spell the ruin of the values you wish to see flourish, such flouting of realism is a price one is forced to pay. In bringing men and women to a fruition which they are unlikely to achieve under their own steam, comedy takes pity on their infantile helplessness and vulnerability. Since history quite often gets things wrong, comedy is needed to correct its deficiencies.

There is also the very different case of Brechtian theatre, in which a prohibition on empathy allows us to relativise any particular perspective and see our way critically around the action as a whole. A certain detached appraisal, alert to conflict and contradiction, is here the enemy of absolute claims. The audience must be denied emotional identification, but only so that it is free to pass critical judgements in the name of a greater compassion, one which concerns not the theatre but political society at large. The comedy of such drama lies not so much in wit or humour as in the structural irony by which one viewpoint is played off against an antithetical one, contradictions are laid bare, a range of possibilities at odds with the actual is intimated, and (as in the so-called alienation effect) one acts and objectifies one's acting at the same time. Devices of this kind have a certain dialectical quality to them; indeed, Brecht once remarked that he had never found anyone without a sense of humour who could understand dialectical thought. Such thought is not in the least inimical to entertainment. 'The theatre of the scientific age', he writes,

> is in a position to make dialectics into a source of enjoyment. The unexpectedness of logically progressive or zigzag development, the instability of every circumstance, the joke of contradiction and so forth: all these are ways of enjoying the liveliness of men, things, and processes, and they heighten both our capacity for life and our pleasure in it.[18]

These are the words of a playwright who claimed that he wanted to make thinking a real sensuous pleasure. 'There is no better starting point for thought than laughter,' writes Brecht's first great champion, Walter Benjamin. 'Speaking more precisely, spasms of the diaphragm generally offer better chances for thought than spasms of the soul.'[19] Since Brechtian drama lays bare the mechanisms by which it achieves its effects, thus breaking the spell of realist illusion, the audience no longer needs to invest psychological energy in maintaining that illusion and can expend it instead in critical appraisal. It is a relief equivalent in its own way to laughter.

For Brecht as for Bakhtin, there is also something inherently comic in the fact that history is mutable and open-ended. The ultimate act of comic inversion is political revolution. Hitler as housepainter yesterday and chancellor today foreshadows the process by which he may be dead in a bunker tomorrow. The opposite of comedy is destiny. In this sense, Brecht's comic aesthetic differs sharply from the fatalism of the cosmic vision. All this, to be sure, overlooks the fact that if despotism is unstable, so are justice and comradeship. Even so, Brecht's point is that even a change for the worse reminds us of the possibility of a change for the better. It is as though the dialectic is the ironic wit of history. For Marxism, there is something darkly comic about the fact that the capitalist class is its own gravedigger, just as there is an incongruous humour in the prospect of the wretched of the earth coming to power. For Hegel, history reveals a similarly comedic structure, as a gap between motive and action, intention and outcome, desire and satisfaction, proves to be the very motor of human progress. Incongruity – the fact that things go awry, slide out of place, spin out of synch – is in this view what sustains the unfolding of Spirit. Gillian Rose writes of Hegel's *Phenomenology of Spirit* as 'a ceaseless comedy, according to which our aims and outcomes constantly mismatch each other, and provoke yet another revised aim, action and discordant outcome'.[20] There is a dissonance at the heart of history, yet one without which it would stall. One might add that those like Brecht who are capable of finding Hegel comic would presumably have no problem in chortling at *Phèdre* or the *Medea*.

It is worth noting that comedy does not need to be funny, any more than wit has to be. There are not many gags in *The Tempest*. Chekhov is comic but not funny, though he began his career as an author of farce and humorous journalism. We laugh when the absurd Malvolio enters cross-gartered in *Twelfth Night*, but not at the lovers' imbroglio in *A Midsummer Night's Dream*. Classically speaking, comedies are narratives in which things go entertainingly awry and are then patched up. Calamities impend and are triumphantly averted. Our infantile, wholly reasonable demand that our tears should be wiped away is fictionally fulfilled, as the Gospel promises that it will be for real in the New Jerusalem. The comic is full of mishaps and pratfalls, but given time and a touch of magic they will all be resolved. As John Roberts remarks, comedy bears witness to 'the endless capacity of humans to work through misrecognitions, errors and misconstruals, as a condition of the recovery and renewal of truth'.[21] Indeed, without this constant deferral and deviation, the truth will fail to reveal itself. In Hegel's view, error and misrecognition are built into the business of its self-disclosure. Tragedy, Søren Kierkegaard argues in his *Concluding Unscientific Postscript*, turns on irresolvable contradictions, and comedy on resolvable ones. None of this, however, need have us rolling helplessly in the aisles. Few people have been carried out of a production of *The Country Wife* or *She Stoops to Conquer* clutching a burst blood vessel.

Sándor Ferenczi acknowledges the force of the superiority theory, but holds that comedy as a form of solidarity with flaws and failings is more fundamental: 'The essence of laughing: How I should like to be as imperfect as that! The essence of laughing at: How satisfactory it is that I am so well behaved, not as imperfect as that! . . . Behind every laughing at there is concealed unconscious laughing.'[22] On this view, ridiculing someone else serves to mask the fact that we, too, would enjoy the freedom to parade our imperfections. It would be gratifying to indulge such inanities ourselves, if only we were not so fearful of social censure. So it is that in Plato's *Republic*, Socrates, himself a kind of philosophical buffoon, points out that we relish the spectacle of others indulging in the preposterous antics we would secretly like to engage in ourselves. It is true that we also resent such people's insouciance, which is part of what leads us to scorn them despite this covert rapport. Even so, we feel for the Fool even as we deride him, partly because his display of folly allows us a certain vicarious easing of psychic pressure.

In the early years of BBC Radio, a producer wrote to an obscure Anglican vicar in a rural parish asking him to give a talk at Easter. The fee, he added, would be five pounds. The vicar wrote back to say that he would be delighted to deliver such a talk, and that he was enclosing his five pounds. If we smile condescendingly at the vicar's naivety, we also sympathise with it. The ego, pleasantly unchallenged, no longer feels the need to assert itself and might even come to confess its own frailties. Oscar Wilde's 'I can resist everything but temptation', like any cavalier display of moral weakness, allows us for a moment to undo the defences we normally erect to conceal our own shortcomings. It is this mental relaxation that makes us smile. Even so, those who cannot keep their blemishes decently hidden, but parade them like a suppurating wound, cause us to jeer but also to wince. We fear for them at the same time as we thrust them firmly at arm's length. Perhaps by some curious contagion their shameless self-display will incite us, too, to drop our guard. If we cringe at the clownish David Brent of *The Office*, it is partly because we are terrified of our own more disreputably infantile impulses; but while we are dismayed to see them put so brazenly on show, we are also secretly delighted, rather as we covertly admire the way in which Brent is insulated by his colossal egoism from an awareness of his own fatuities.

The superiority theory is right that we smile at others' imperfections, but wrong to assume that this is simply because we enjoy looking down our noses at them. All the same, there is no doubt that a good deal of humour involves insult and abuse. With the cruel hounding of Malvolio, Shakespeare's *Twelfth Night* sails perilously close to shedding its festive aura. The same goes for the sadistic mistreatment of Shylock. There are jokes which mock women, as in this vignette of God, a woman, creating the universe: 'Darkness covered the face of the earth. And God said, "Let there be light", and there was light. And God said: "Er – could I just see the darkness again?" ' To which a suitable feminist riposte might be: 'What do you call the useless bit at the end of the penis? – The man.' There is a similar dusty answer to the question 'What do you call a black man who flies a plane?' 'A pilot, you racist bastard!'

The Irish have been known to savour anti-Irish jokes ('What's a Kerryman's foreplay?' 'Brace yourself, Brigid'), while Jews are not slow to recount anecdotes against themselves such as the following: Goldberg is stranded on a Swiss mountain as the storm clouds close in, and a Red Cross team of dogs, paramedics and mountain rescue experts are in anxious pursuit of him. 'Mr Goldberg,' they shout through the mist, 'where are you? It's the Red Cross!' A faint voice is heard to cry back: 'I've given already!' The same Goldberg is strolling along a riverbank with his adult son when the son loses his footing and slips into the water. 'Help!' Goldberg shouts. 'My son, the lawyer, is drowning!' Or think of the gag about the benefits of dementia, the first being that you get to hide your own Easter eggs, the second being that even though you're married you can have a new sexual partner every day, and the third being that you get to hide your own Easter eggs. There is also a cartoon of a band of pensioners on a protest march raising the cry of 'What do we want?' 'What do we want?' Jokes of the kind are intended as amicable rather than abusive, but the line between the two is not always clear. They may express a genuine aggression which they simultaneously disown, one to which the victim cannot object without appearing humourless ('It's only a joke!'). Trapping the target in this untenable situation may be part of the fun.

It is possible to feel superior to oneself, as in Groucho Marx's immortal quip, 'I wouldn't join a club that let in people like me.' Thomas Hobbes holds that to laugh at oneself is always to jest at some past, inferior self, but this is not true of Groucho's words.[23] The joke simultaneously builds him up and puts him down, placing his higher self at a disdainful remove from his lower. Not to want to associate with people like himself reveals a degree of good taste which people like himself sorely lack. The gag is pathetic in its self-denigration, but also in its feeble effort at superiority. Yet self-denigration, not least for Jews like Groucho, may be a survival tactic. To declare oneself worthless may be to proclaim that one is not even worth killing. Your murderers would only succeed in making themselves look ridiculous, thus sinking to one's own degraded level, and one is good-heartedly concerned to save them from this indignity. To take another's demeaning view of you and flaunt it yourself may succeed in disarming them. In this sense, self-deprecating humour may register one's subservience as part of a strategy for surmounting it. If the ego cowers humbly enough, it may escape the brutal upbraidings of the superego. At least one has enough insight and resilience to be ironic at one's own expense. What transcends one's mediocrity is the candour with which one confesses it. *Qui s'accuse, s'excuse.* The English are particularly adept at putting themselves down, as in the suggestion (in line with their supposedly unrevolutionary spirit) that if they ever decide to drive on the right, they shall do so gradually.

In *Absolute Recoil*, Slavoj Žižek endorses Alenka Zupančič's dismissal of the standard view that comedy is a question of human frailty and finitude tripping up our more noble pretensions.[24] On the contrary, comic art for both Žižek and Zupančič involves not finitude but a curious kind of immortality, a cartoon-like capacity to survive the most devastating of calamities. You fall from a precipitous height, dust yourself down and spring up to resume the chase. Yet this view of the comic is not entirely at odds with the frailty and finitude thesis. On the contrary, it is precisely the Fool's lowly, humble, imperfect status, his debunking of all grandiose idealism, that invests him with an odd kind of immortality. Those who can fall no further enjoy a strange kind of invincibility. It is as though a tough-minded awareness of mortality endows you with a wisdom which allows you to rise above it. To be conscious of one's own limits is to transcend them. It is the inconspicuous who can outflank death, while the high and mighty are riding for a fall. The genre that portrays this hubris is known as tragedy. What survives indefinitely is sheer meaningless matter, which like the imperishable common people of Bakhtinian carnival has all the blind persistence of the death drive.

We are speaking, then, of an immortality of biology rather than of the spirit, as is clear if we glance once again at *Waiting for Godot*. Vladimir and Estragon are unable to hang themselves, since to imagine them dead would be inconceivable. There is not enough life in them for that. They are simply not up to such metaphysical profundities as ceasing to exist. They cannot even muster the resolution they would need to do away with themselves, since to extinguish one's will requires a strenuous act of will. There is no death in this drama, or indeed in Beckett's work in general. Instead, there is simply a steady physical and moral disintegration, one too banal and inconspicuous to meet with anything as definitive as a conclusion. These are subjects too feeble even to assume their own finitude, and as such the polar opposite of the classical tragic protagonist. By freely appropriating his own death and defeat, the tragic hero can transcend his finite status and weave something eternally precious out of the rags of time. The comic character, by contrast, achieves not eternity but immortality, in the sense of infinite survival. He just goes on and on. For some, such a 'bad' infinity, as Hegel would call it, is a vision of hell.

The superiority thesis fails to account for the fact that, as with so-called joking relationships in certain tribal societies, insults may be a form of friendship. They serve to show the resilience of a human bond, which is well able to withstand such barbs. It also overlooks the difference between laughing at someone's jokes and laughing at *them*. Even if jokes themselves are exercises in offensiveness, a dubious enough proposition, our relation to the comedians who tell them involves more than a conspiracy of contempt. We laugh at them partly because we enjoy sharing some congenial communication, even if the jokes themselves happen to be put-downs. No humour that involves such a relationship can be simply superior. It is true that such a rapport is not always easy to come by. Many sorely misguided men and women have chuckled at the gags of Bob Hope, but it would have taken a supremely charitable audience to find the man himself in the least amusing. All one needs for such humour is a slick style and a posse of well-paid scriptwriters. This, however, was not the case with Tony Hancock, Eric Morecambe or Frankie Howerd, as it is not true of Larry David, Eddie Izzard, Ricky Gervais or Steve Coogan. In all these cases, the source of humour is at least as much a style of life, way of seeing or oddball personality as it is the isolatable joke. It is also worth noting that even when comedians like David, Gervais and Coogan present themselves as objects of mockery, our amusement at their antics is always in part the enjoyment of a skilful performance, and is thus never simply denigratory. One recalls Samuel Johnson's wise reminder that the spectator of a play never forgets for a moment that he or she is in a theatre.

Part of the humour of a comedian like Frankie Howerd springs from the meta-commentary by which he continually makes sardonic reference to the script, the audience, his own performance, the performance of his fellow actors and so on. This allows us to relax the effort of make-believe by which we are supposed to assume that this man is not a performer, that his words are spontaneous and not scripted and that his inter-actions with the other actors are real-life ones. We know, to be sure, that none of this is true, as Johnson points out about a theatre audience; but fiction and drama nonetheless demand a provisional suppression of this truth if they are to achieve their effect, and when the effort of suppression is no longer required, the energy we invest in it can be expended in laughter. The Brechtian alienation effect, by which an actor makes it clear through a deliberately 'staged' performance that he is an actor and not a real-life individual, also allows us to economise in this way. In Brecht's case, however, we direct what we save not into laughter but into a process of critical reflection on the action the play presents.

Even when we do get a rise out of the ridiculous, our response is often enough an ambiguous one. In a work like *Joseph Andrews*, the novelist Henry Fielding is especially amused by the practice of moral virtue, since good-heartedness in a world as predatory as ours is hard to distinguish from sheer gullibility. If the virtuous are to cope with the corrup-tion that besets them on all sides, they must be aware of it – but then how can they still be unblemished? Anyway, is not their innocence partly responsible for provoking the wicked-ness of others? Fielding's novels thus turn their satire on the unworldly victims of vice at the same time as they scold those who perpetrate such depravity; but this is not to say that they do not admire their blamelessness as well. The naive may be comic, but they are also rather touching, as well as being a good deal preferable to the hard-boiled. We smile at the guile-less and maladroit not only because we look down on them but because we commend their uprightness, however absurdly otherworldly it may appear, as well as feeling pleasantly unthreatened by them. We love the other, comments Jacques Lacan, in so far as he or she is lacking, and we smile because he embodies our own defects, not simply by contrast with our own completeness. Comedy, writes George Meredith a touch too charitably, is a stranger to contempt. You must, he insists, reveal the folly of men and women without loving them any the less, and give a semi-caress to those you sting.[25]

The superiority theory raises some intriguing questions about the status of language. If jokes are forms of verbal rather than physical aggression, does this defuse or intensify their pugnacity? Is being insulted or abused preferable to a punch on the nose, or should one take the point of the old adage that sticks and stones will break my bones but names will really hurt me? A word can destroy a career, a reputation or even an individual more easily than a blow. Banter and joshing may seem innocuous enough, but they belong to a continuum that stretches to vile abuse. Yet would any abuse be too vile for those who commit genocide or bring hundreds of thousands to financial ruin? Are verbal onslaughts similar to the ritual behaviour by which some of the other animals avoid actual combat, or are they a potentially mortal form of such combat? Shakespeare's Hamlet sees words as mere idle tokens, but there are Shakespearian plays in which the word of a monarch can slice off a head. Words are mere breath, but they can extinguish breath as well. How can language be at once mere sign and material force?

Fortunately, there is a good deal more to humour than spite and rancour, as we shall now go on to see.

3

INCONGRUITIES

There are many theories of humour in addition to those we have looked at. They include the play theory, the conflict theory, the ambivalence theory, the dispositional theory, the mastery theory, the Gestalt theory, the Piagetian theory and the configurational theory.[1] Several of these, however, are really versions of the incongruity theory, which remains the most plausible account of why we laugh. On this view, humour springs from a clash of incongruous aspects – a sudden shift of perspective, an unexpected slippage of meaning, an arresting dissonance or discrepancy, a momentary defamiliarising of the familiar and so on.[2] As a temporary 'derailment of sense',[3] it involves the disruption of orderly thought processes or the violation of laws or conventions.[4] It is, as D. H. Munro puts it, a breach in the usual order of events.[5] The philosopher Thomas Nagel's list of absurdities – your trousers falling down while you are being knighted, declaring your love to a recorded message, a notorious criminal becoming president of a philanthropic organisation, and so on – are for the most part examples of incongruity.[6] (Nagel might have added to his list a US secretary of state guilty of conducting illegal warfare being awarded the Nobel Peace Prize, a classic instance of *comédie noire*.) Children under the age of two, so the psychologists inform us, will laugh at incongruous sights.[7] The peekaboo game, which children find funny even when only a few months old, is one of the earliest cases of incongruity, as one appearance is rapidly replaced by another. Children, insists Freud, lack all sense of the comic, but it is possible he is confusing them with the author of a notoriously unfunny work entitled *Jokes and Their Relation to the Unconscious*.

In his poem 'The Pleasures of the Imagination', the eighteenth-century poet Mark Akenside remarks that

Where'er the power of ridicule displays
Her quaint-ey'd visage, some incongruous form,
Some stubborn dissonance of things combin'd,
Strikes on the quick observer[.][8]

The theme is taken up by the eighteenth-century scholar James Beattie, who argues in his *Essays on Poetry and Music* that we laugh at whatever is composed of heterogeneous parts – though humour can also arise, he maintains, from an unexpected similitude. Some forms of incongruity, he admits, are not amusing, but this is because their comicality is outweighed by some other feeling (pity, fear, disgust, admiration and the like). Incongruities can also be easily defused and domesticated, thus ceasing to entertain us. 'There are few incongruities,' Beattie writes, 'to which custom will not reconcile us.'[9] They are, moreover, culturally variable, so that 'all the nations on earth are in some particulars of dress or deportment mutually ridiculous to each other'.[10] It is also possible, he argues, to be amused by incongruities of which we morally disapprove, rather as there are politically incorrect jokes which are actually quite funny, or accomplished works of art with dubious ideological overtones.

Both Kant and Schopenhauer link laughter with incongruity. In his *Critique of Judgment*, Kant writes rather quaintly of how 'to a sudden shift of the mind, first to one and then to another point of view for considering its object, there can correspond an alternating tension and relaxation of the elastic portions of the intestines which communicates itself to our diaphragm',[11] with the consequence that our lungs expel air in the form of laughter. Physical and psychological motions are directly coupled, in a way that links the incongruity theory to the release thesis. In Schopenhauer's *The World as Will and Representation*, the dissonance at stake is one between the concept of an object and our sensory perception of it. In what one might dub an epistemological theory of humour, a sense

69

of the ludicrous arises from subsuming an object under an inappropriate concept, or under a concept which is appropriate to it from one viewpoint but not from another. One may also achieve a comic effect by subsuming different objects under the same notion.

There is also an element of superiority at work here. Schopenhauer views the Will, a category which for him includes the bodily, instinctual, perceptual, self-evident, spontaneous and gratifying, as locked in permanent combat with Reason or the Idea; and humour arises when Reason, unable to cope with the intricacies of perceptual experience, has its limits thrown momentarily into relief. In an epistemological version of the Fool upending the Master, the comic thus represents the momentary triumph of the lowly Will over the abstract Idea – or, in Freudian parlance, the id over the superego. If this is an agreeable victory, it is not least because for Schopenhauer as for Freud, Reason censors and represses our sensory enjoyment. It is therefore gratifying, Schopenhauer remarks, to see that 'strict, untiring, troublesome governess, the Reason' momentarily worsted. In this sense, one might claim, there is a touch of *Schadenfreude* in all humour, even when it is not amusement at another's distress. It is our own prized rationality we take a poke at. The person whose discomfort yields us pleasure is oneself.

The Victorian philosopher Herbert Spencer champions the incongruity theory in an essay on the physiology of laughter, though we have seen already that he backs the discharge hypothesis as well.[12] Charles Darwin claims that laughter is caused by 'something incongruous or unaccountable, exciting surprise',[13] but holds that there is generally some strain of superiority in our chuckling as well. Like a number of thinkers, then, he links two different hypotheses of humour. So does Sigmund Freud, though in his case the views in question are the release and incongruity theories. We have seen already how humour in Freud's view involves a lifting of repression, but he also associates it with a coupling of incompatible features. Rhyme, for example, links different words phonically together, and is thus in Freud's view a species of wit.

In an essay entitled 'The Comic', Ralph Waldo Emerson sees humour in inherently bathetic mode as a clash between ideal and actual, or conception and execution. It involves, he maintains, a perception of discrepancy. Robert L. Latta regards it as resulting from a series of rapid cognitive shifts which involve the relaxation of the mind and hence the production of laughter – though since such shifts need not in his view involve incongruity, he distinguishes his case from standard incongruity theories.[14] J. Y. T. Greig views laughter as resulting from sudden oscillations between, say, pleasure and pain, or from one idea or emotion to a dissimilar one.[15] In *The Act of Creation*, Arthur Koestler treats humour in similar style as springing from a conflict of incompatible frames of reference,[16] while John Morreall regards it as depending on sudden sensory, conceptual, perceptual or emotional shifts.[17] In *The Odd One In*, Alenka Zupančič finds a prime source of comedy in the way different versions of the world refuse to slot together, as we veer between mutually exclusive interpretations. In her view, there is a kind of fissure, enigma or contradiction in the human condition from which laughter can spring, as indeed there is for Jonathan Swift. Humanity, writes Swift's colleague Alexander Pope, is glory, jest and riddle, and jest precisely because it is riddle.

Comic incongruity has a lengthy history. In the Book of Genesis, Abraham falls on his face and laughs when God tells him that despite his advanced years he will have a son. His son's name, Isaac, means 'the laughing one', as though the child is tickled by the sheer improbability of his own existence. Abraham's elderly wife Sarah is equally amused by the prospect of her geriatric pregnancy. Despite its august biblical backing, however, the incongruity theory is not without its problems. The Victorian author Alexander Bain is one of a range of thinkers to point out that by no means all incongruities are amusing. Snow in May is one of Bain's examples, as is, rather more comically, 'the multitude taking the law into its own hands', which in his view is no occasion for chortling.[18] Michael Clark seeks to resolve the problem by claiming that the incongruities we find comic are those we enjoy for their own sake, rather than for any ulterior motive.[19] Surrealism, for example, is not funny because it is designed to disconcert, rather than revelling in absurdities as an end in themselves. Yet one could presumably treat the idea of snow in May as an end in itself, whatever that might mean, without thereby turning it into a piece of humour. (In any case, there are depressing ecological reasons why it is considerably less incongruous today than it was in 1875, when Bain published his book. What is dissonant at one time or place need not be so at another.) Incongruity, Clark maintains, is a necessary but not sufficient condition of humour, but this is surely question-able. On the contrary, it would seem neither necessary nor sufficient – not necessary because there are forms of humour which in no very conspicuous sense involve incongruities; not sufficient because not all such discrepancies are enough to provoke laughter. Some types of incongruity are alarming or disgusting, unpleasant or plain unfunny. Suddenly sprouting another head is unlikely to induce a fit of giggles in your family and friends.

Another problem with the thesis is the elastic nature of the concept of incongruity, which with a touch of ingenuity can be made to cover a multitude of conditions. It is up to the reader to decide from the discussion that follows whether the concept is an impressively capacious one, or whether it can too easily be stretched beyond all usefulness. Take, for example, the mildly amusing story of Moses descending Mount Sinai with the tablets of the Law tucked under his arm. 'I've got them down to ten,' he bawls to the assembled Israelites, 'but adultery's still in!' The comic disparity here turns on the idea of Moses as a trade union official, bargaining with the Almighty on behalf of his disgruntled rank and file. This, however, is a different type of discordance from the one to be found in a recent announcement by the Royal Navy. Having replaced the customary bunk system in one of its new battle-ships with individual beds and cabins, the Navy proudly proclaimed that this was the only one of its vessels in which every sailor slept in his own bed. In advertising its up-to-dateness, it succeeded in implying that the service was rife with homosexual promiscuity.

This type of dissonance involves a gap between what is said and what one means to say, as with the old anti-Soviet joke that 'Capitalism is the exploitation of man by man, whereas communism is just the reverse.' In both cases, an official meaning releases an informal one comically at odds with it. Another piece of black humour from the former Communist world, one which also involves incongruity, turns on the contrast between the Soviet Union and the slightly more relaxed form of Stalinism then in power in Yugoslavia: 'In the Soviet Union, party officials drive cars while the people walk, whereas in Yugoslavia the people themselves drive cars through their elected representatives.'

'You've got to stop masturbating,' a doctor tells his patient. 'Why?' asks the patient. 'Because I'm trying to conduct a medical examination,' replies the doctor testily. This, too, relies on a sense of incongruity, as we slip without warning from one frame of reference (masturbating in general) to another (masturbating here and now). 'How come there's only one monopolies commission?' plays on an apparent self-contradiction. Or take the anecdote of the British army officer in the Second World War who asked a Gurkha sergeant to instruct his men to jump from an aircraft at one thousand feet. The sergeant consulted with his men and returned to the officer with the verdict that they regarded the jump as too dangerous. Instead, they were prepared to jump from five hundred feet. Dismayed by this apparent failure of nerve in a famously plucky breed, the officer warned the sergeant that at five hundred feet his men's parachutes would not have time to open. 'Oh, you mean we have parachutes?' asked the sergeant. The incongruity here revolves on a conflict of assumptions, as well as on the Gurkhas' curious readiness to hurl themselves from one unsurvivable height but not from another.

There is a similar slippage of frameworks in the story of a visitor being shown by a guide around a Moscow art gallery and pausing before a painting entitled *Lenin in St Petersburg*. Inspecting the canvas more closely, the visitor can see only a portrayal of Lenin's wife, Nadezhda Krupskaya, in bed with a handsome young member of the Central Committee in a Moscow bedroom. 'But where is Lenin?' asks the visitor bemusedly, to which the guide replies, 'Lenin is in St Petersburg.'

Our expectation that the title of the painting will describe what it represents has to be abruptly revised, as we realise that 'Lenin in St Petersburg' alludes to one of the reasons for the scene depicted, not to the scene itself. Or take this brief snatch of dialogue:

A: I'm off to see that film about the *Titanic*.

B: Oh, it's marvellous – especially the bit at the end when it sinks.

A (*sarcastically*): Oh, thanks very much!

The incongruity here is plain: how could anyone know about the *Titanic* without being aware of the single most salient fact about it? Perhaps we also feel a mildly sadistic frisson at the discomfiture of the second speaker, who has unwittingly given away the movie's plot, as well as at the indignation of their amusingly ignorant companion. Embarrassment (other people's, at least) mixes pleasure and pain. Ignorance of the *Titanic*, incidentally, is not confined to jokes. A friend of mine who used to work as a guide in the Titanic museum in Belfast found herself being constantly approached by puzzled Americans who couldn't understand why a museum should be dedicated to a movie.

A quick slide of meaning, shift of perspective or sudden baulking of expectations can occur at a purely verbal level, as in ' "The Duke's a long time coming today," said the Duchess, stirring her tea with the other hand', in which the latter phrase forces us suddenly to revise the meaning of the former. The same is true of 'The first few days were the hardest, as the teenage boy said of his visit to a nudist camp.' 'Would you like a bridal suite?' a young man asks his bride-to-be while planning their honeymoon, to which she replies, 'No thanks, I'll just hang on to your ears.' 'Have you read Marx?' 'Only where I sit down' is another such example. In Dorothy Parker's retort to being told that revellers at Halloween duck for apples – 'There, but for a single consonant, is the story of my life' – this process rises to self-consciousness. It is what Max Eastman calls 'holding out a meaning and then snatching it away'.[20] Incongruity begins to merge here into wordplay and ambiguity. Like irony, however, ambiguity can itself be ranked as a form of incongruity, as two divergent meanings collide in an economy of difference-and-identity.

The same goes for puns, the lowest form of comic life, as in 'A guy drowned in a bowl of muesli. A strong currant pulled him in.' Even with such feeble contrivances, the mind is allowed to freewheel for a moment, rather as it is in Kant's theory of art, relishing the economy created by a coincidence of meaning, the enigma of two terms being one or one term being two, and the sense of enlargement and free capacity which a sudden modulation of sense may bring. We shift from the rigours of the cognitive to a state in which we can shuck off the logic of cause and effect, or the law of non-contradiction, and savour the ludicrous or irreconcilable for its own sake. We are no longer constrained by the axiom that everything is itself and not another thing, and the release of this restriction can take the form of laughter. If the ego invests in unity, identity and univocity, the id is enamoured of fragments, non-sense, part-objects, multiplicities and non-identities, all of which are bound from the ego's viewpoint to appear incongruous or absurd; and a joke occurs when the ego dips for a moment into this outlandish element. It is in the nature of the reality principle to keep the mind focused by thrusting other possibilities at arm's length, and in the nature of humour to allow them to swarm in.

The disruption of expectations, sometimes by a single word, is a familiar form of incongruity – Oscar Wilde's 'Nothing succeeds like excess', for example, or his complaint that 'I live in constant fear of not being misunderstood.' 'The young people of today have no respect for dyed hair' is another such Wildean shaft, where all is pitched on a single epithet. A Freudian slip is when you say one thing and mean a mother. The *fin de siècle* poet Ernest Dowson once declared that absinthe makes the tart grow fonder. The famously bibulous playwright Brendan Behan described himself as a drinker with a writing problem. In all these cases, the sense of a word or phrase is comically askew to the one we are geared up to expect. Language is in and out of place at the same time, as we are forced to hold a conventional meaning in tension with a semantic twist. Dorothy Parker's crack 'The transatlantic crossing was so rough that the only thing I could keep on my stomach was the First Mate' is a case in point. The sign one sometimes used to see on public garbage cans, 'Refuse To Be Put In This Basket', alters its meaning in accordance with which syllable of 'Refuse' one stresses. In addition to the absurdity of being solemnly admonished not to allow oneself to be stuffed into a rubbish bin, we smile at the way an official notice, with its faintly intimidating aura, is momentarily divested of its authority and made to look foolish. Incongruity and superiority thus conspire together. One might always claim, however, that discrepancy is not the same as incongruity. The latter is a question of a thing being inappropriate, incompatible, out of keeping, which need not be true of all discrepancies.

On the subject of individual words, one is reminded of the tale of the man who went into hospital demanding to be castrated. After seeking fruitlessly to argue him out of this perverse desire, the medical staff finally succumbed to his wishes and removed his testicles in a lengthy surgical operation. The patient was wheeled back to his ward, and on recovering from the anaesthetic asked the patient in the next bed what operation he was waiting for. 'Circumcision,' the man replied. '*That's* the word!' exclaimed his newly castrated companion, ruefully slapping his forehead. The joke, which no doubt causes the male of the species to squirm rather more than the female, illustrates among other things how disproportionateness is a type of incongruity.

Aristotle speaks in *Rhetoric* of humour as springing from the violation of verbal expectations, while Cicero remarks in his treatise on oratory that the most common kind of joke is when one thing is expected and another said. It is through this small rupture of logic that laughter can well up. A minor change of punctuation can comically deflect an intended meaning. 'The batsman's Holding, the bowler's Willey', a BBC radio cricket commentator once announced, innocently unaware that the removal of the comma yields a different sense entirely. Even a shift of tone can signal an abrupt reversal of perspectives, as with the man who, when reminded that two negatives make a positive but that the opposite does not hold, responded with a wearily sceptical 'yeah, yeah'. A good deal of Woody Allen's humour hinges on incongruity:

'There's no question that there's an unseen world. The problem is, how far is it from mid-town and how late is it open?'

'I don't want to achieve immortality by my work. I want to achieve it by living on in my apartment.'

'Not only is there no God, but try getting a plumber at weekends.'

'One of the thieves [on Calvary] was saved,' writes Samuel Beckett in *Malone Dies*. 'It's a generous percentage.' This is glumly comic because the discourse of theology sits cheek by jowl with the language of accountancy, the gravitas of the one deflated by the profanity of the other. Bathos or debunkery is in this sense a mode of incongruity, as high and low are yoked discordantly together. Yet deviations can also be ranked as types of incongruity, since they call to mind a norm in the act of transgressing it, thus confronting us with a tension between the two. In fact, the word 'humour' originally means one whose temperament diverges from the norm. People may laugh at deformities not only, or not at all, out of a sense of superiority, but because they are incongruities. We smile at the oddball and eccentric because it disrupts our stereotypical expectations. Henri Bergson, for whom such aberrations are to be corrected rather than celebrated, combines both superiority and incongruity theories. In his view, the social rigidity that humour is out to chastise can be seen as a form of incongruity, since it means not fitting in with prevailing conventions. Bergson's own organicist ideology, by contrast, is set on welding together things which split and clash.

One form of such inflexibility is monomania. Why is Schopenhauer's unremitting gloom so funny? Not because there is anything in the least entertaining about his world view, but because to cling to a thesis through thick and thin, refusing all compromises or concessions, seeking perversely to extend it to the most implausible of cases, is the conceptual equivalent of the eccentric, who stubbornly refuses to be anything but himself. Excessive consistency is as ruinous to a sound sense of reality as categorical chaos. In *Tristram Shandy*, Tristram's own inability to unify his experience is simply the inverted mirror image of his father Walter's crazed system-building.

Doublings and repetitions can be incongruous, since there are certain phenomena – human beings, for example – we expect to be inimitable, and our expectations are thrown out of gear when they turn out not to be. The two weeping secretaries is a case in point. There are other cases in which what seems to be one is actually two, as with the man who inquired of a renowned musicologist whether the correct pronunciation of a certain composer's name was Schu*bert* or Schu*mann*. The riddle of two-in-one, one might claim, also lifts the mildly repressive logic involved in distinguishing rigorously separate identities, and in doing so moves us to laugh, as we do at an accomplished impersonation. We are able to economise on our psychological expenditure, as we could not if two quite different phenomena were to claim our attention.

Repetition for Bergson is a mechanising device, one that smacks of intractability. Instead of acting creatively, one blindly repeats, as in certain forms of neurosis, and this is comic in the sense that monomania is comic. One reason why mimicry or mimesis can be funny is because it is a form of repetition, implying an identity between items that are really distinct. Yet we also smile at the skill with which mime, parody or twists of irony are executed, which is a different source of enjoyment. We experience the mild elation one feels at the spectacle of anything dexterously done, which compounds the comic effect. Besides, a deft performance allows us to economise on the effort we expend in appreciating it, as a laborious one would not. When it comes to impersonation, there may also be a mildly aggressive element at work: 'Look, I can be you just as well as you can – even better, maybe. You're not so special after all.'

If there is something comic (as well as at times a little eerie) about doublings, so is there about the *sui generis*. Indeed, the word 'peculiar' means both specific or particular and weird, quirky, offbeat. Our drive to classify may be thwarted by a grotesque mismatching of objects, but it is equally baffled by things that refuse to be categorised and which, therefore, like some of Dickens's freakish figures, present us with the conundrum of that which is purely itself. There is something enigmatic, even unnerving, about the wholly self-identical. The word 'humour' originally refers to this type of idiosyncrasy, which as we shall see later has played a privileged role in English culture. To humour someone is to indulge their whims and foibles, an act which may be morally admirable; yet if men and women were not so feeble and foolish, they would not need such cosseting in the first place. In this sense, humouring belittles humanity at the same time as it constitutes a commendable example of it.

Another type of incongruity is defamiliarisation, in which one holds in tension a common meaning and a circuitous version of it. The Irish writer Flann O'Brien's 'Catechism of Cliché' provides a rich storehouse of examples:

What inexpensive unrationed commodity is often said to exceed the man possessing it in value? – His salt.

What does one sometimes have it on? – The most unimpeachable authority.

On what article manufactured in Switzerland are hypochondriacs, paranoiacs and the like continually to be found? – The watch.

What (I ask in astonishment) do you do at the same time as you tell me so? – Mean to stand there.

Into what must all the facts be taken? – Consideration.

How is money measured when there are enormous quantities of it in question? – In relation to the surplus available for incineration.

Who is one every bit as good as? – The next man.

What completely non-existent thing is frequently stated to be still there? – The nothing more that often remains to be said.

In what direction does the meeting break in disorder? – Up.

What act did I perform in relation to him with long lengths of narrow fabric? – I had him taped.

To what obscure cardiac shellfish is heat imparted by the sight of the national flag flying over the Old House in College Green? – It warrums the cockles of me heart.[21]

A harmless parlour game is to invent examples of one's own:

Through what mutually contrasting consistencies must one persevere? – Thick and thin.

What rhetorical query as to the denominational affiliation of the Bishop of Rome expresses a sardonic response to the self-evident? – Is the pope a Catholic?

Why will their parents prepare them for rest at an unusually early hour of the evening? – Because they're tired little teddy bears.

As constricted as the anus of which small rodent are the inebriated? – A mouse.

With what item of equipment of a long, flat-bottomed boat does one refuse to effect tactile contact with him? – A bargepole.

To test out the incongruity theory, let us take three real-life comic situations. An American anthropologist friend of mine was driving rather too fast in the west of Ireland when he was stopped by a police officer. 'What would you do,' the officer asked him, leaning ominously into the driver's window, 'if you were to run into Mr Fog?' For an enthralling moment my friend thought that he had stumbled upon a lost tribe in Connemara which personified the weather, speaking of Master Sunshine, Mrs Hailstone, Brother Thunder and so on. Quickly abandoning this hypothesis, he decided that the officer was simply being patronising and replied with heavy sarcasm 'Well, I guess I'd put Mr Foot on Mr Brake.' Whereupon the policeman looked at him strangely and growled, 'I said *mist or fog.*'

Another friend of mine once spent a semester as a visiting professor at a university in West Africa where there were a number of peacocks on the lawn. Returning to the campus some years later for a brief visit, he was strolling with the vice-chancellor when he noticed that the peacocks were no longer in evidence. 'What have you done with the peacocks?' he asked the vice-chancellor, and then, feeling a little waggish, added, 'You haven't eaten them, have you?' The vice-chancellor turned a grave countenance towards him and replied, 'Dr and Mrs Peacock left for London last month.'

Finally, an anecdote concerning myself. I was browsing in an Oxford bookshop when I noticed a display of *Made Simple* books – *German Made Simple*, *Chemistry Made Simple*, and so on. A friend of mine, a distinguished Oxford philosopher, was standing beside the bookstand, leafing through the *Philosophy Made Simple* volume. Seizing the chance of a jape, I crept up behind him and murmured into his ear, 'That's a bit difficult for you, isn't it?' He swung round in alarm, and my first thought was that he had undergone cosmetic surgery. Then I realised that it was not my friend at all. It was a complete stranger. Muttering a hasty apology, I scampered out of the store. Somewhere in the world there is a man who believes people in Oxford are so odiously elitist that they jeer openly at total strangers seeking to improve their minds.

All these situations involve incongruities of one kind or another: a clash of meanings, the inappropriateness of a police officer apparently indulging in toddler talk, the grotesque disparity between a polite chat with one's host and the outrageous implication that he and his colleagues are cannibals, and the inaptitude of apparently sneering for no good reason at a complete stranger. Yet in none of these cases is incongruity the driving force of the humour. The release theory surely accounts for the comic effect far better. We laugh because we are able to free ourselves from the straitjacket of convention and vicariously indulge our glee in the chutzpah of cheeking a figure of authority or being abominably rude. In each case, there is a sadistic or masochistic element at work, as we relish the discomfort of others, or even (as in the bookshop incident) of oneself. It is satisfying as well as distressing to see another humiliated, partly because it bolsters our own infirm egos, partly because, as we have suggested already, it grants us some vicarious indulgence of our own vulnerabilities.

It is worth noting that a fair amount of what we find funny is (to borrow a Freudian term) overdetermined, meaning that it is the product of a multiple range of factors. A joke may combine the pleasurable unconstraint of wordplay, nonsense or ambiguity with an unseemly collision of concepts, a bathetic jolt from high to low and a vindictive animus against some hapless victim, as well as yielding us a degree of aesthetic pleasure by its aptness and concision and by the skill with which it is executed.

A good deal of humour is a question of transgression or deviation. As the boundaries between different phenomena blur, we are able to relax our rigorously taxonomising impulse, and the energy we conserve in doing so is discharged in laughter. This can be true of irony, bathos, puns, wordplay, ambiguity, incongruity, deviation, black humour, misunderstandings, iconoclasm, grotesquerie, out-of-placeness, doubling, absurdity, nonsense, blunders, defamiliarisation, quick changes and hyperbole. Mutually incompatible possibilities which the reality principle must exclude in order to maintain a degree of order and coherence come welling up in a minor outbreak of anarchy, as the world suddenly ceases to be as self-consistent as it appeared a few moments ago. If this is pressed too far, the result can be an alarming loss of bearings. Pleasure, accordingly, begins to shade into distress.

I have included incongruity in the list of comic devices just provided, but there is a sense in which most of them can be subsumed under that heading. And that this is so leads one to wonder once again how useful such a commodious concept can be. Another problem with the incongruity theory is that it is descriptive rather than explanatory. It tells us what we laugh at, but not why we do so. What is needed, then, is to splice the incongruity thesis with the release theory, which is indeed an explanatory move. We have seen that there are theorists who yoke the superiority to the incongruity theory, or couple the former with the release theory, but release and incongruity would seem the most fruitful combination of cases. To formulate more fully, then, what I have suggested already: humour happens for the most part when some fleeting disruption of a well-ordered world of meaning loosens the grip of the reality principle. It is as if for a moment the ego is able to relinquish its grim-lipped insistence on congruence, coherence, consistency, logic, linearity and univocal signifiers, ceases to fend off unwanted meanings and unconscious associations, allows us to revel in a playful diversifying of sense and causes us to release the psychic energy conserved by this bucking of the reality principle in a smile or a snort of laughter. It is notable that Freud, the primary exponent of the release theory, does not quite forge this connection. It is the psychical energy we expend in repressing the obscene and aggressive which claims his attention in the joke book, not for the most part the unconscious labour involved in maintaining a shapely, coherent sense of reality.

One of the finest of all comic novels, Laurence Sterne's *Tristram Shandy*, puts this disintegration of the reality principle brazenly on show. Unable to maintain the unity and consistency of his narrative, not least because of the disruptive incursions of the unconscious and the need to leave absolutely nothing out of his account, Tristram's narration finds itself adrift in a potential infinity of text, shuttling from one elaborate digression to the next, nipping from one time scheme to another, sinking under a surfeit of signification and unable to say one thing without saying half a dozen others simultaneously. The more faithfully the hero seeks to record his life history, the more he is obliged to present us with a monstrous mass of information under which the novel begins to buckle. One representation spawns another and that another, until the narrative logjams and starts to come apart at the seams. Comic realism is unmasked as a contradiction in terms, since realism is inevitably repressive, as eloquent for what it doesn't say as for what it does, and such exclusivity is at odds with the all-embracing spirit of comedy. In his faux-tender concern not to cheat on his readers by shaping and editing his story, Tristram succeeds with thinly disguised sadism in plunging them into utter confusion. This catastrophic collapse of the reality principle, one which pressed far enough ends up in madness, is prototypically comic.

In a remarkably perceptive essay entitled 'On Wit and Humour', the early nineteenth-century critic William Hazlitt is already to be found hooking up the release and incongruity theories. He speaks of 'the habitual stress which the mind lays upon the expectation of a given order of events, following one another with a certain regularity and weight of interest attached to them', and of how 'the ludicrous, or comic, is the unexpected loosening or relaxing of this stress below its usual pitch of intensity, by such an abrupt transition of the order of our ideas, as taking the mind unawares, throws it off its guard, startles it into a lively sense of pleasure, and leaves no time nor inclination for painful reflections'.[22]

This, in effect, is Hazlitt's pre-Freudian version of the lifting of psychic repression. The essence of humour, he insists, lies in 'the incongruous, the disconnecting one idea from another, or the jostling of one feeling against another',[23] and this sudden clash or dislocation produces a mental spasm or disruption which expresses itself in the physical convulsion of laughter. It is an anti-dualist conception of the comic, one for which the mental and physical are as inseparable as a sleeve and its lining. 'The mind having been led to form a certain conclusion,' Hazlitt remarks,

and the result producing an immediate solution of continuity in the chain of our ideas, this alternate excitement and relaxation of the imagination, the object also striking upon the mind more vividly in its loose unsettled state, and before it has time to recover and collect itself, causes that alternate

91

excitement and relaxation, or irregular convulsive movement of the muscular and nervous system, which constitutes physical laughter. The discontinuous in our sensations
produces a correspondent jar and discord in the frame.[24]

Much the same process, as we have seen, is true for Kant.
Hazlitt also recognises that there can be a perverse element in
humour, as the very prohibition of laughter serves simply to
provoke it. It is for this reason that 'we can hardly keep
our countenance at a sermon, a funeral, or a wedding'.[25] As
psychoanalytic theory is aware, the Law incites desire rather
than simply repressing it. It tempts us to transgress so that it
can punish us for our aberrations.

Delighting in dissonance is not in Hazlitt's view to be
unequivocally encouraged. 'To be struck with incongruity in
whatever comes before us,' he warns, 'does not argue great
comprehension or refinement of perception, but rather a loose-
ness and flippancy of mind and temper, which prevents the individual from connecting any two ideas steadily or consistently
together.'[26] Genteel wit is one thing, but giddiness is quite
another. As we shall see in the next chapter, there is always a
problem with comedy about how far you can go before an
admissible bout of high spirits escalates into verbal or conceptual
anarchy.

However productive the incongruity theory may have
proved, we are no nearer to explaining why we laugh at some

forms of out-of-placeness and not at others. What the philosophers called category mistakes (imagining the soul as an invisible bodily organ, for example) involve incongruities, but few of them are causes for hilarity. Nor have we cast light on why utterances and situations apparently free of such discord can still be funny. There are also jokes which involve incongruity but draw primarily on the primitive pleasures of abuse, as when the journalist Christopher Hitchens remarked that George W. Bush's eyes were set so close together that he could have used a monocle rather than a pair of glasses. So humour has not yielded up all of its secrets, and the sizeable academic industry devoted to investigating it may roll on unperturbed.

4

HUMOUR AND HISTORY

The governing elites of ancient and medieval Europe were not greatly hospitable to humour. From the earliest times, laughter seems to have been a class affair, with a firm distinction enforced between civilised amusement and vulgar cackling. Aristotle insists on the difference between the humour of well-bred and low-bred types in the *Nicomachean Ethics*. He assigns an exalted place to wit, ranking it alongside friendship and truthfulness as one of the three social virtues, but the style of wit in question demands refinement and education, as does the deployment of irony. Plato's *Republic* sets its face sternly against holding citizens up to ridicule and is content to abandon comedy largely to slaves and aliens. Mockery can be socially disruptive, and abuse dangerously divisive. The cultivation of laughter among the Guardian class is sternly discouraged, along with images of laughing gods or heroes. St Paul forbids jesting, or what he terms *eutrapelia*, in his Epistle to the Ephesians.[1] It is likely, however, that Paul has scurrilous buffoonery in mind, rather than the vein of urbane wit of which Aristotle would have approved.

Mikhail Bakhtin comments that 'laughter in the Middle Ages remained outside all official spheres of ideology and outside all official strict forms of social relations. Laughter was eliminated from religious cult, from feudal and state ceremonials, etiquette, and from all the genres of high speculation.'[2] The oldest monastic rule we know of forbade joking, while the Rule of St Benedict warns against the provocation of laughter, an impertinence for which St Columbanus imposed the penalty of fasting. The medieval church's dread of comedy leads to murder and mayhem in Umberto Eco's novel *The Name of the Rose*. Aquinas is typically more relaxed about the matter in his *Summa Theologiae*, recommending humour as a form of therapeutic play of words or deeds in which nothing is sought beyond the soul's pleasure. It is necessary, he believes, for the solace of the spirit. Indeed, a reluctance to engage in humour counts in his eyes as a vice. For Christian theology, the pointless delight of a joke reflects the divine act of Creation, which as the original *acte gratuit* was performed simply for its own sake, driven by no necessity and with no functional end in mind. The world was fashioned just for the hell of it. It is more like a work of art than an industrial product.

This churlish suspicion of humour sprang from more than a fear of frivolity. More fundamentally, it reflected a terror of the prospect of a loss of control, not least on a collective scale. It is this that in Plato's view can be the upshot of excessive laughter, a natural bodily function on a level with such equally distasteful discharges as vomiting and excreting. Cicero lays out elaborate rules for jesting and is wary of any spontaneous outburst of the stuff. The dissolution of the individual body in laughter might presage a popular riot, and medieval carnival – a species of social revolution in fictionalised, fantastic, strictly sporadic form – sailed close enough to such comic chaos to justify these anxieties. The plebeian body is perpetually in danger of falling apart, in contrast to the disciplined, suavely groomed, efficiently regulated body of the hygienic patrician. There is also a dangerously democratic quality to laughter, since unlike playing the tuba or performing brain surgery, anybody can do it. One requires no specialised expertise, privileged bloodline or scrupulously nurtured skill.

Comedy poses a threat to sovereign power not only because of its anarchic bent, but because it makes light of such momentous matters as suffering and death, hence diminishing the force of some of the judicial sanctions that governing classes tend to keep up their sleeve. It can foster a devil-may-care insouciance which loosens the grip of authority. In its carnivalesque mode, it may also breed a phantasmal sense of immortality, one that dispels the sense of vulnerability essential for the maintenance of social order. Even Erasmus, author of the celebrated *In Praise of Folly*, also penned a treatise on the education of schoolchildren which warns of the perils of laughter. The work admonishes pupils to press their buttocks together when farting to avoid excessive noise, or to mask the unseemly sound with a well-timed cough.

The playwright William Congreve complains in 'An Essay Concerning Humour in Comedy' of the sort of comic spectacles that force him to entertain demeaning thoughts about his own nature. He could never look very long upon a monkey, he reflects, without feeling deeply mortified. Parodies, mimicries and aberrations remind one of the alarming fragility of one's norms. In similar spirit, Joseph Addison claims in a piece in *The Spectator* that Laughter is the daughter of Folly, who married Frenzy, the son of Nonsense, whose mother was Falsehood. It is not the most heartening genealogy for those fond of a giggle. The eighteenth-century critic John Dennis holds that humour is chiefly to be found among the menial classes. Since it is a question of the body rather than the mind, it is more likely to flourish among the uneducated, whose reason has not learnt to suppress their animal instincts. In an essay on 'A Comparison between Laughing and Sentimental Comedy', Oliver Goldsmith similarly associates comedy with the base and mean. This prejudice against humour was inherited, most improbably, by Shelley, who is said to have remarked in conversation that there could be no complete regeneration of humankind until laughter is put down.[3] It is a grim prospect when even radical libertarians look askance on humour.

The eighteenth-century philosopher David Hartley rejects out of hand 'low similarities, allusions, contrasts, and coincidences, applied to grave and serious subjects, that occasion the most profuse laughter in persons of light minds; and weakens reverence for sacred things'.[4] Too much wit and mirth, he holds, frustrate the search for truth by preventing our minds from perceiving the true nature of things. In similar vein, the Victorian novelist George Meredith looks to humour for 'mental richness rather than noisy enormity'[5] and is keen to distinguish refined laughter from the kind of 'brutish' comedy that 'roll[s] in shouting under the divine protection of the Son of the Wine-jar'.[6] Much comedy is low, buffoonish stuff, whereas literature is an elevated affair; so is a comic literature a contradiction in terms? Is a theory of comedy equally oxymoronic? We can measure degrees of refinement, Meredith informs us, by the 'ring of the laugh', a claim that returns us to the starting point of this study. Fishwives cackle, while statesmen chuckle.

For all his prissiness, Meredith is one of the few theorists of humour before the twentieth century to venture into the realm of gender. A good deal of comedy, he maintains, revolves on the battle of the sexes, and plays a vital role in elevating women from 'pretty idiots' to admirable wits. What he sees as the lack of comedy in the East springs in his view from the low status of women in that sector of the globe. Where women have no freedom, he insists, comedy is bound to be absent. There can be no genuine civilisation without sexual equality, and 'there will never be comedy where civilisation is not possible'.[7] In the absence of such civility, the comic spirit is 'driven to the gutters of grossness to slake its thirst'.[8] Where women are reduced to household drudges, the form of comedy tends to be primitive; where they are tolerably independent but uncultivated, the result is melodrama; but where sexual equality thrives, the art of comedy flourishes alongside it.

The resistance to comedy in the early modern age belongs for the most part to the history of Puritanism.[9] Yet one might argue that Thomas Hobbes's morose theory of humour is as inimical to the thing itself as the most crop-headed scourge of theatre and popular festivity. The background to the Hobbesian hypothesis is the violence, antagonism and partisanship of civil war, along with the emergence in the seventeenth century of the doctrine of possessive individualism. It is into this unlovely vision of men and women as anti-social animals driven largely by power and appetite, solitary, self-interested creatures locked in ferocious mutual contention, that even the apparent innocence of mirth and laughter is drawn.

Something of this sombre outlook informs the lacerating, splenetic satire of the early eighteenth-century Tory old guard, of Pope and Swift and their conservative colleagues, with their urge to taunt, deface, ludicrously inflate or hack brutally down to size. Yet the key shift of sensibility in this period is one away from this corrosive satire towards a more cordial world view. Determined to put the political strife and ideological rancour of the previous century behind it, the prevailing climate in the clubs and coffee houses is one of serenity and affability, a blitheness of spirit that will come in time to characterise the English gentleman. We are witness to the rare phenomenon of humour, or at least good humour, moving close to the centre of a dominant ideology. Cheerfulness and congeniality usurp a surly Puritanism. Indeed, an aversion to earnestness will typify the English upper classes all the way to the era of Oscar Wilde, where being earnest in one sense of the word (the term at the time could be a code word for 'gay') is to be relished far more than earnestness in its common-or-garden meaning. If jesting and raillery are implicitly political for the eighteenth-century clubmen, it is among other things because it is the tight-lipped zealot and sectarian bigot that these apologists for conviviality have in their sights. Good humour, one might claim with only a touch of hyperbole, is a counterblast to revolution.

For the Earl of Shaftesbury, to practise the comic spirit is to be easy, natural, flexible and tolerant rather than stiff-necked and fanatical. Humour is a splendid palliative for 'superstition and melancholy delusion'.[10] Satire, with its coarse belliger-ence, is a cultural residue of a more abrasive, agonistic world, and is now to be tempered by a good humour and eirenic spirit which spring from the genteel classes' belief in their own inexhaustible benevolence. Men and women are to be seduced rather than censured into virtue, humoured rather than harangued. As the historian Keith Thomas remarks, the early eighteenth century is a period when 'humour grows kindly and . . . bizarre quirks of personality are not aberrations calling for satiric attack but amiable eccentricities to be savoured and enjoyed'.[11] Hegel notes in his *Philosophy of Fine Art* that in modern comedy, imperfections and irregularities are objects of entertainment rather than disdain. For the eighteenth-century Tory satirists, by contrast, aberrations from a common human nature are potentially dangerous anomalies to be whipped back into line, which is not to say that they may not be sources of entertainment as well. One can find such a double optic in the work of Ben Jonson. For a less censorious literary art, by contrast, oddballs are causes of genial amusement, as with *The Spectator*'s Sir Roger de Coverley, Fielding's Parson Adams or Sterne's saintly Uncle Toby. Congreve defines humour as 'a singular and unavoidable manner of doing, or saying anything peculiar and natural to one man only; by which his speech and actions are distinguished from those of other men'.[12]

'Unavoidable' is worth underlining. Humour in this sense of the word is really a form of determinism. Since it is part of one's character, given rather than chosen, it follows that to upbraid men and women for their oddities is illogical. To speak of 'men and women', however, is not quite

appropriate, since in Congreve's view humour is a phenomenon confined largely to men – indeed, to Englishmen.
Women, given the natural coldness of their natures, tend
to be deficient in the stuff. The point, anyway, is that the
comic is now well-nigh synonymous with the idiosyncratic.
In fact, it is becoming hard to distinguish from the sheer fact
of individuality itself. If humour means the inimitable flavour
of a particular personality, then all individuals are humorous,
though some are more so, in the sense of more freakish,
anomalous or curmudgeonly, than others. And since individuality is to be valued, a peculiarly English indulgence of
such foibles ('It takes all kinds to make a world'; 'It'd be a
funny world if we all thought the same') is beginning to
burgeon.

The humour in question, to be sure, is a refined, genteel
affair, as these pub clichés are not. In this sense, as we have
seen, eighteenth-century authors can be quite as reproving of
belly laughs as their Puritan predecessors. One should never
be heard to laugh, Lord Chesterfield admonishes his son in a
letter. It was widely rumoured that neither Swift nor Voltaire
went in for such uncouthness. (Samuel Johnson, by contrast,
was reputed to be an inveterate chuckler.) Genuine wit
provokes a smile rather than a roar, thus testifying to the
supremacy of the mind over the servile senses. Humour is a
question of the body, while wit is a faculty of the soul. The
essayists Joseph Addison and Richard Steele advocate a sober,

polite vein of mirth, though sobriety was not otherwise Steele's strongest point. Humour was to be sanitised and gentrified, for fear of clowning and buffoonery.

Much of the cult of congeniality flourished on the Gaelic fringes of the nation, where social relations were rather less subject to the creed of possessive individualism, and where notions of communality could still flourish. In the harsh conditions of life of the Scottish Highlands or the west of Ireland, human relations were rather less rationalised, bureaucratised, commercialised and anonymously administrated than they were at the metropolitan centre. The Gael may have been stereotyped as a brawling barbarian, but he was also the very model of sociability. A description of Oliver Goldsmith, who hailed from the Irish midlands, fits the caricature perfectly:

His generous warmth of heart, his transparent simplicity of spirit, his quick transitions from broadest humour to gentlest pathos, and that delightful buoyancy of nature which survived in every depth of misery, – who shall undertake to separate these from the Irish soil in which they grew, where impulse predominates still over reflection and conscience, where unthinking benevolence yet passes for considerate goodness, and the gravest duties of life can be overborne by social pleasure, or sunk in mad excitement?[13]

It is interesting to note how the compliment grows steadily sourer as it unfolds, until what began as patronising praise ends up as a rap over the knuckles. Here, with a vengeance, is the Gael with a twinkle in his eye and a smile on his lips, though with one hand wrapped a little too tightly around the ale jug. The Dublin-born Richard Steele, despite being of English descent, was also said to display the stereotypically Irish qualities of liveliness, good humour and jovial companionship, and like his compatriot Oliver Goldsmith found the English a touch churlish and farouche. Both authors, however, claimed to detect hearts of flesh beneath their stony exteriors. The average English citizen, Steele maintains in an excess of generosity, conceals under his rough air and aloof behaviour a bleeding compassion and womanish tenderness, while Goldsmith believes that his adopted fellow citizens, though outwardly ill-natured, have hearts that sympathise with every distress.

Gladys Bryson points out that some Scottish Enlightenment theorists contrast a social order founded on kinship and custom with one based on more impersonal relations, and find for the most part in favour of the former.[14] 'Sociability, not individualism,' observes another commentator, 'was the critical ingredient in the Scottish definition of sensibility.'[15] Society was not to be seen as a contractual affair à la Hobbes and Locke, but as an extension of the domestic unit, and thus as natural to human beings. It was the need to preserve a sense of community and moral economy in an increasingly self-interested social order that inspired some thinkers north of the English border to sing the praises of the cooperative virtues. The Scottish philosopher Adam Ferguson gloomily contrasts the solidarity of a tribal or clan-based culture with the 'detached and solitary individuals' of modern commercial society. In the latter conditions, he argues, malice, envy and competition sunder the bonds of human affection. Despite this, he is still able to believe, in anti-Hobbesian spirit, that 'love and compassion are the most powerful principles in the human breast'.[16] His colleague Adam Smith, travestied in our own time as a flint-hearted free marketer, also regards the spirit of commerce as debilitating, and both he and Ferguson espouse what Bryson calls 'an ethics of feeling'.[17] Smith is an enthusiast of the compassionate or empathetic imagination, and thus as much preoccupied with spiritual as with commercial exchange. To empathise with others is to put oneself in their place. We can trade ourselves, as well as our commodities, with our fellow citizens, and in the eighteenth-century Man of Feeling, this responsiveness to another's distress or delight has evolved into a well-nigh pathological cult of sensitivity.

So it was that a philosophy which hymned the virtues of kinship, benevolence and solidarity crept into the metropolis from regions that were still to some extent pre-modern – places in which the power of sentiment, the authority of tradition and the social role of personal affinities were fighting a rearguard action against economic individualism and the sovereignty of law over custom. It is a problem for capitalist social orders that their calculative rationality risks dispelling the consensus of feeling needed to support and reproduce their own social relations, and a judicious importation of such sentiment from the Gaelic margins, duly polished and refined, could be pressed into this cause. If the political state is reduced to a utilitarian contract, while individuals are seen as solitary, self-motivating atoms, the need for such a shared sensibility and stout framework of value, one within which competitive individualism can be given free rein without risk of disruption, is all the more pressing. Sentiment, amiability and good humour will oil the wheels of commerce. The eighteenth-century novelist Henry Brooke, author of an extraordinarily tedious piece of fiction entitled *The Fool of Quality*, writes of how the merchant 'brings the remotest regions to neighbour-hood and converse . . . and thus knits into one family, and weaves into one web, the affinity and brotherhood of all mankind'.[18] In more radical circles, by contrast, the cult of sympathy could threaten to derail this whole project in the name of some less crassly egoistic vision of social existence.

In Brooke's sanguine view, the proliferation of commercial relations among men will bring in its wake a deepening of their mutual sympathies, which in turn will render the conduits of commerce all the more smooth and efficient.

Commercial intercourse breeds politeness, cements social relations and knocks the rough edges off the philistine bourgeois by infusing him with a touch of aristocratic grace. The extension of trade and the spread of fellow feeling are mutually enriching. Montesquieu, whose *De l'esprit des lois* lies behind much of this philosophy of *le doux commerce*, has a touching faith in the civilising power of bills of exchange. Commerce renders you more docile and gregarious; and since this kind of wealth is diffuse and mercurial, it is less easy for an autocratic state to confiscate or control. The Scottish philosopher John Millar even ropes the proletariat into this corporate well-being: when labourers are massed together by the same employment and by regular intercourse, he claims, they 'are enabled, with great rapidity, to communicate all their senses and passions', and the basis for plebeian solidarity is thus laid down.[19] Society works by a certain pleasurable, instinctual cooperation, and a vital metaphor for this communality is sharing a joke.

Peace, politeness, good humour and sociability are now to be seen as the foundation of prosperity. The old-style patrician values of honour, *hauteur* and military glory must yield to the middle-class virtues of meekness, civility, familial harmony and social affections. It was, one critic comments, 'the end of an heroic age and the beginning of a sentimental one'.[20] In the work of the greatest Scottish philosopher, sentiment lies at the source of all moral judgement. What distinguishes a real from an imaginary object in David Hume's view is simply a different intensity of feeling. Pity, pathos and the pacific, all values of which women are seen as the chief custodians, must be translated from the domestic to the public sphere. The Irish philosopher Edmund Burke is a leading spokesman for this strategy. There is a new turn to sentiment and cordiality, to the tender and uxorious. Sensibility becomes a kind of rhetoric of the body, a semiotics of blushing, weeping, fainting and palpitating.

Richard Steele, whose journal *The Tatler* was a formidable force in shaping this new cult of manners, pens letters to his wife full of such impeccably polite swoonings. She is his 'Dear Creature', 'Dear Ruler', 'Dearest Being on Earth', and in one such missive he signs himself 'Yr Affectionate Tender Oblig'd Husband & Lover'. These scrawled, scrappy notes, peppered with allusions to God, Truth and Love, sometimes arrive with a gift of tea or the odd guinea. In a letter to inform his wife that he is dining with Lord Halifax, he adds, 'I dye for thee I languish.'[21] 'I have long entertained an ambition to make the word Wife the most agreeable and delightful name in nature,' Steele gushes in the fortieth edition of *The Spectator*. There is a new brand of manliness in the making, one hostile to false wit and aristocratic libertinage, wedded to the virtues of truth, meekness, simplicity, good sense, non-violence, generosity of spirit and connubial affection. The empathetic imagination – a quick, intuitive sense of how others are feeling – belongs with this feminised sensibility. God, Steele argues in *The Christian Hero*, has fashioned for us a common nature which 'presses us by natural society to a closer union with each other . . . and by a secret charm we lament with the unfortunate, and rejoice with the glad; for it is not possible for a human heart to be averse to anything that is human; but by the very mien and gesture of the joyful and distressed we rise and fall into their condition'.[22] Joy, he adds, is 'communicative', rather as jesting is. For Francis Hutcheson, too, we are as naturally stirred to joy by the sight of another's magnanimity as we are nauseated by a foul stench or enraptured by a sublime prospect. Moral judgements are as swift and spontaneous as physical reflexes.

It was thus that humour, sympathy and high spirits came to play a central role in a whole programme of cultural politics. One of the chief tasks of the republic of letters was to instruct a heavy-handed bourgeoisie in new patterns of feeling, tempering their hard-headedness with an infusion of manners, civility and the domestic affections. The advertisement to the 1780 edition of Laurence Sterne's complete works promises that reading them will foster benevolence in society. Fiction, theatre and periodical journalism were all to be pressed into a campaign to aestheticise social existence by imbuing it with a certain grace, elegance and moral sensitivity, all the way from homilies against duelling to eulogies of commerce. The middle classes were to be refined and the insolent aristocracy domesticated. Moral philosophy was to be retrieved from the clerics and schoolmen and adapted instead to the club, the salon and the coffee house. The new cultural milieu was to be characterised not by frivolity (an upper-class vice) but by a light-hearted nimbleness of spirit that could easily issue in laughter.

Even so, if humour could spring easily from this cultural climate, it is an outlook that cuts deeper than mere joking. It is rather the bright-eyed vision of a social class in the ascendant, increasingly assured and at ease with themselves – a stoutly Protestant phalanx of bankers, lawyers, clerics, landowners, merchants, jobbers, brokers and entrepreneurs who feel (correctly, as it transpired) that history is on their side, and who are busy consolidating their cultural identity along with their land and capital. Buoyed by imperial power, a rapidly expanding economy and a lucrative colonial trade, this emergent middle class regards it as more prudent and profitable to come to terms with the gentry and aristocracy rather than confront them eyeball to eyeball over the barricades. If they have curbed the insolence of the *ancien régime*, they are also unacquainted with the fear of insurrection from below which was to plague their industrial-capitalist inheritors. Humour, benevolence, sentimentalism and a dash of Panglossian self-satisfaction are their feel-good factors. The Whig potentate Shaftesbury draws a startlingly direct connection between the prevalence of wit and free trade: 'liberty and commerce bring (wit) to its true standard', he observes, while restrictions on trade reduce it to a dismally low ebb.[23] Both comedy and wit, he maintains, have political implications as well as economic ones. In their generous, open-hearted, free-minded quality, they can subvert the autocratic and authoritarian.

Rather as Hobbes's speculations on laughter reflect a more general world view, so does Francis Hutcheson's riposte to them. It is becoming impossible, Hutcheson complains with Hobbes in his sights, to appeal 'to the old notions of natural affections, and kind instincts, the sensus communis, the decorum and honestum'. Instead, everything is a matter of selfishness, and 'laughter itself must be a joy from the same spring'.[24] Hutcheson is scandalised by the view that self-interest lies at the source of human action, and speaks up instead for a less bloodless conception of human behaviour. 'Men,' he writes, 'approve deeply that beneficence which they deem gratuitous and disinterested.'[25] 'As soon as any action,' he remarks, 'is represented to us as flowing from love, humanity, gratitude, compassion, a study of the good of others, and a delight in their happiness, although it were in the most distant part of the world, we feel joy within us, admire the lovely action, and praise its author.'[26] The advocates of self-interest can never account for 'the principal actions of human life such as the offices of friendship, gratitude, natural affection, generosity, public spirit, compassion'.[27]

Lurking beneath Hutcheson's approach to comedy is a remarkably buoyant view of human nature, not least for an Ulster Presbyterian minister. The whole of his writing is a broadside against philosophical egoism. The notion of *Schadenfreude*, so central to later thinkers such as Nietzsche and Dostoevsky, can find no foothold in his kindly, innocent ethics. Our minds, he maintains, show a strong bias 'toward a universal goodness, tenderness, humanity, generosity, and contempt of private goods'.[28] Virtue in his view includes 'an inclination to cheerfulness, a delight to raise mirth in others, which procures a secret approbation and gratitude towards the person who puts us in such an agreeable, innocent, good-natured, and easy state of mind, as we are conscious of while we enjoy pleasant conversation, enlivened by moderate laughter'.[29] The harbinger of the kingdom of God is now less the church than the dining club. Goodness and sensual enjoyment are intimately interwoven, and benevolence is a kind of robust bodily pleasure. One savours the delectability of acts of kindness as one might smack one's lips over a succulent dish of prawns.

In the blithe Hellenism of a newly self-confident middle class, the benevolent citizen and the bon viveur are becoming hard to tell apart. Hutcheson's compatriot Laurence Sterne, who hailed from Tipperary, speaks of the 'glorious lust' of doing good. Virtue is selfless, profitless, gratifying and gratuitous. It lies beyond all self-serving calculation, and like the aesthetic constitutes its own reward. In all these ways, it is at odds with marketplace rationality, an affront to a social order for which nothing can exist for its own self-delight. This vein of virtue is the foe of all Puritan self-repression, and laughter is its outward sign. Such laughter is the kind of utterance that the linguisticians would call 'phatic', meaning one focused on the act of communication itself. One laughs not over this or that, but to show that one rejoices in the company of another and intends them no harm – that one is not, for example, about to launch into a brutally candid critique of their character and physical appearance – while the other laughs in turn, elated at this amicability but also intent on conveying the same message. We take pleasure in pleasing the other, but also in letting them see that we are well disposed to them and wish to entertain them, an enjoyment which is increased by the other's glad response to our good humour and by their similar desire to be agreeable. It is thus that in a self-generating process, mutual laughter tends to foster yet more mutuality. Social lubrication of this kind is in fact laughter's most common function, more so than the telling of jokes.[30] Good humour, so the sociologists inform us, is more pervasive than humour. Susanne Langer points out that whereas humour needs an object, laughter, which may spring simply from one's pleasure in the company of others, does not.[31] Kundera writes somewhat similarly in *The Book of Laughter and Forgetting* that there is a kind of laughter without an object, an 'expression of being rejoicing in being'. When the audience of a comedy roars with laughter, they are responding to a situation on stage but also to each other's high spirits, delighting in this solidarity of sound and the momentary fellowship it fosters. The Freudian jest, a mere sportive piece of wordplay, is comedy of this kind – though not the joke, which in Freud's view is fuelled by ulterior motives.

For Hutcheson, humour springs not from condescension but precisely from the implosion of such lordly attitudes – from the puncturing of inflated grandeur and the bringing low of the mighty. It represents 'none of the smallest bonds of common friendship',[32] and as such is a foretaste of the eternal festivity of the kingdom of God. If it anticipates a world of sensuous fulfilment to come, however, it is also, like the church, an instrument for attaining it, creating concord where there was previously solitude and estrangement. Nothing is more instantly communicative, Hutcheson remarks, than a good joke. The joke is now a metaphor for a whole set of amicable social relations, and as such is a profoundly political utterance. If it is an earthly version of divine caritas, it is also the prototype of a more companionable society. The world, as Laurence Sterne reminds us, is big with jest, of which his own literary art is one of the many midwives; and for an author like Hutcheson, what this pregnant planet it is labouring to deliver is a more comradely social order. It is a republic of free and equal citizens that the bonhomie of the club or dinner table prefigures. In the fourth volume of *Tristram Shandy*, Sterne speaks of his ambition to construct 'a kingdom of hearty laughing subjects'. To laugh together is to share a bodily as well as spiritual communion, one whose closest analogy is a festive meal. In this unity of the physical and mental, laughter is a refutation of Cartesian dualism. There is no point to this reciprocity beyond its own self-delight, which is why it has a certain affinity with art. Humour of this kind is an implicit critique of instrumental rationality. It exists purely for the joy of the contact.

Not all of Hutcheson's parishioners were enraptured by his progressive views. One disgruntled member of his church, cheated of his weekly dose of hellfire by the minister's liberal-minded sermons, described him as a 'silly loon' who had babbled to them for an hour about a good and benevolent God without a single word about the comfortable old doctrines of election, reprobation, original sin and death. That the man is so little known today is something of a scandal. He was the father of Scottish philosophy, a thinker who taught David Hume much of what he knew and deeply influenced the early writings of Immanuel Kant. In the hands of his pupil Adam Smith, his economic thought helped to lay the foundations of the modern world. He was a full-blooded republican who took a radical line on the right of the oppressed to overturn an unjust ruling power. He was also a seminal influence on Thomas Jefferson, and thus a leading intellectual actor in the

American Revolution. Some of his ideas were then imported back into his native Ireland in the form of the insurrectionary doctrines of the United Irishmen. He championed the rights of women, children, servants, slaves and animals, spoke up for marriage as an equal partnership, denounced patriarchal power, was tried for heresy in Glasgow and displayed a remarkably enlightened attitude to non-Western cultures. He even put in a good word for aliens.

The cult of benevolence did not go unchallenged. If humour is an image of the good life, then virtue must be as spontaneous as laughter, in which case how can it be a question of merit? Goodness becomes instinctive, and though we may be loved for it we cannot be complimented on it. Besides, doesn't this reduce right action to a kind of whimsy? Is one to be compassionate simply when one feels like it? It would seem on this theory that we can no more help sympathising or commiserating with others than we can help plucking a finger from a flame or spotting a hippo in one's field of vision. 'Merely to be struck by a sudden impulse of compassion at the view of an object in distress,' writes one commentator tartly, 'is no more benevolence than is a fit of gout.'[33] There is a danger of subjectivising morality away, of which the moral traditionalists of the age are deeply wary. '[The sentimentalists'] generous notions,' writes Sir John Hawkins sardonically, 'supersede all obligation: they are a law to themselves, and having *good hearts* and abounding in the *milk of human kind-*

ness are above those considerations that bind men to that rule of conduct which is founded in a sense of duty.'[34] Samuel Taylor Coleridge was later to remark in his *Aids to Reflection* that the mischief perpetrated by Sterne and his sentimentalist disciples outweighed all the evil inflicted by Hobbes and the materialist school. Goldsmith, who approved of benevolence but disliked sentimentalism, felt much the same: true generosity, he insists, is a moral duty with all the force of law, a rule imposed upon us by reason rather than a matter of what happens to take our fancy.[35] The comment is in line with the New Testament view that love in the sense of caritas or agape has very little to do with feeling. Its paradigm is the love of strangers and enemies, not friends or family members. In any case, benevolence as a social ideology was not to survive. At a later stage of their evolution, in the throes of industrial capitalism and imperial warfare, the European middle classes were to come up with a somewhat less sprightly version of human nature. Freud's joke book, which like much of his work reverts in some sense to a Hobbesian image of humanity, is a case in point.

Roughly speaking, good humour is a matter of smiling, while sentimentalism is a question of mingling your smiles with tears, and thus a mildly masochistic affair. One finds an agreeable pathos in human adversity, rather as for the eighteenth-century aesthetician the experience of the sublime involves a sense of rapture at the prospect of being crushed and overwhelmed. Gratified by his own fine feelings, the sentimentalist flaunts them like so many emotional commodities. Benevolence and the empathetic imagination are centrifugal faculties which bear you beyond yourself, whereas sentimentalism is secretly centripetal, a self-regarding condition in which you luxuriously consume your own sensations. It is really a devious form of narcissism, in which one sympathises with one's own act of sympathising. The Man of Feeling is a moral pelican who feeds off his own inner stuff. The object of one's delight or distress is simply an occasion for the reified emotions to which it gives rise. As John Mullan observes, 'the intensity of a special experience of feeling' in the eighteenth century 'was a substitute for common and prevailing sympathies'.[36] Sentimentalism makes a fetish of feeling, overreacting to a social order which makes too little of it. The sentimentalist and the utilitarian are sides of the same coin, as Marx considered the Romantic and the utilitarian to be. 'Sensibility', as the age called it, can be a kind of pathology, a mark of the neurasthenically overbred. In Sterne's *A Sentimental Journey*, Yorick dreams up images of affliction in order to savour the orgasmic pleasures of pity. The Irish novelist Lady Morgan bemoans in her *Memoirs* her 'unhappy physical organisation, this nervous susceptibility to every impression which circulated through my frame and rendered the whole system acute',[37] but she is really just boasting of how compassionate she is. The destitute and disabled are a heaven-sent opportunity for exercising your philanthropy. As William Blake recognised, pity generally implies that the catastrophe has already happened, and that there is precious little beyond lamentation that you can do about it.

It is this current of sentimentalism that will pass into the nineteenth century. We have seen that there is a difference in eighteenth-century culture between the benevolent and the sentimental – between, say, Fielding and Steele, or Goldsmith and Sterne. Dickens, by contrast, finds it hard to be the one without the other. Henry Fielding is convinced that virtue is natural to humankind, while appreciating its ludicrous aspects and suspecting in his tough-minded way that folly and roguery are a good deal more prevalent, whereas there is little of such moral sinew in Dickens's sensibility. One of his hallmarks as a novelist, however, is a distinctive blend of the sentimental and the grotesque, two literary modes that pull in opposite directions. If sentimentality trades in the mainstream emotions of pity, pathos, tenderness and the like, the grotesque deals with the freakish, deviant and offbeat. The novels sometimes blend the two by being stirred to a tear and a twinkle by sheer amiable eccentricity.

A good many Dickensian figures are humorous in both modern and medieval senses of the word – uproariously comic, yet comic on account of their striking idiosyncrasies. Nor is this quirkiness simply funny. It can be as alarming as it is amusing. Dickens's eccentrics tend to be bound tight in the straitjacket of their own temperaments, compulsive, obsessive and pathologically repetitive, a prey to their own unbending personalities, free to be themselves yet slaves to their own singularity. Some of his characters perform their identities like a piece of street theatre, their selfhood all mask and surface, while with others the self is an enigma buried inaccessibly out of sight. His oddballs, by contrast, tend to be notoriously poor actors, unable to swerve from what they are, stuck in their selfhood like a lifer in his cell. Eccentrics diverge from social norms, yet their behaviour is as predictable as the workings of a steam engine. Their bizarreness can be unnervingly close to madness and monstrosity, or simply to a terrifying brand of egoism. In this atomised social order, men and women occupy their own sealed spaces, their modes of communication opaque or outlandish, their relations often enough a mere interlocking of oddities. Speech is less lucid self-disclosure than just one more capricious feature of an individual, like a trick of gait or twist of the mouth. Characters have their trademark wheedling whine, churlish mumble, quick-fire delivery, pious cant or verbose ramblings. The sensus communis so prized by Addison and Hutcheson has fragmented into an errant individualism, one that is now, ironically, representative of a whole social condition. Some years ago, an Oxford don used to stand at the bar of a pub with a parrot perched on his shoulder, his obvious delight in his own disdain for convention somewhat tempered by his equally obvious fear that the bird might excrete down his shirt front.

What if virtue itself were just another humour, as with the Cheeryble brothers of *Nicholas Nickleby* or Mark Tapley of *Martin Chuzzlewit*? Is warm-heartedness no more than a private whim? Sentimentalism, too, has largely shed its social dimension and has beaten a retreat into the domestic arena, which is now less a microcosm of the public sphere, as it is for Steele and Burke, than a refuge from it, as with Wemmick's moated and fortified suburban home in *Great Expectations*. The festive spirit survives, but it has been for the most part privatised, as a Pickwickian generosity of heart becomes less and less socially effective. By the time we arrive at John Jarndyce of *Bleak House*, the twinkly-eyed, chubby-cheeked philanthropy of the preposterous Cheeryble brothers has declined into a decidedly more muted vein of benevolence. Dissociated from a world of brute fact, feeling is driven in on itself, growing at best self-indulgent and at worst pathological.

All the same, Dickens's fiction continues to look indulgently on human foibles, however sinister or disturbing, and as such takes its place in the mainstream of English comic art. If there is something funny (in the sense of comic) about the funny (in the sense of peculiar), it is because the aberrant is the incongruous. There is a political context to this genial indulgence. In his *Essays on Poetry and Music*, James Beattie holds that humour thrives on idiosyncrasy, and that such

121

peculiarities of temperament flourish most vigorously in a free nation. Despotism, he maintains, destroys diversity, and along with it eccentricity. In non-autocratic societies, individuals are allowed to go their own distinctive ways, and this singularity is conducive to comedy. When men and women are massed together in towns, however, these agreeable foibles disappear, steamrollered by a more uniform style of life. Comedy is thus more a rural than urban affair, the spirit of those who are secluded from sophisticated social intercourse. Even so, Beattie is quick to insist that 'savages' are little given to chuckling, and that wit stages its appearance on the social scene only in civilised monarchical set-ups like his own. Such regimes establish peace, thus lending individuals enough sense of security to pursue both private business and the regular practice of humour. Kings and queens, it would appear, are indispensable conditions for comedy. Besides, in such societies persons of all ranks can freely intermingle in the public sphere, which breeds wit, pleasantries and politeness.

Beattie's ideal social order, then, would seem to be one in which the populace display their charming quirks of character in the rural wilderness, while gentleman coruscate in the metropolitan coffee houses. His strictures on the autocratic state as unfavourable for comedy are echoed two centuries later by Harold Nicolson, who informs us in *The English Sense of Humour* that 'a sense of humour cannot prosper either in a totalitarian or classless society or in a society in process of revolution'.[38] It is indeed a cogent argument against abolishing extreme inequalities of wealth that it is likely to bring wordplay and witticisms grinding to a halt, and one which leftists should doubtless take to heart. What if one were to do away with chortling along with capitalism? Nicolson tells us that he intends to exclude from his reflections any consideration of 'tart', bitter, sardonic, debunking proletarian humour, while claiming somewhat contradictorily that the English all laugh at the same thing regardless of social class. Even so, he is broad-minded enough to point out that 'the propertied classes . . . have a very lively appreciation of cockney humour and regard it with affection'.[39] English humour, he maintains, is characterised by tolerance, kindliness, sympathy, compassion, gentleness, affection, shyness and diffidence. Like the English themselves, it is suspicious of both the intellectual and the extremist, and at its finest is playful, childish, comforting and inoffensive. One suspects that Nicolson would not have been the most devoted fan of Sarah Silverman.

For authors like Sterne and Dickens, humour is among other things a way of keeping a harsh world at arm's length, as well as celebrating comradeship and delighting in the curious and exotic. Sterne's Shandy Hall is a stagnant rural backwater populated by freaks, lunatics and psychic cripples, a sphere of bungled projects, sexual impotence and grotesque misadventures in which laughter is one of the few forms of defence, recompense or transcendence ready to hand. Another is writing itself, which continues to flourish even in these sterile conditions. The state of the human species cannot be as dire as it seems if it can produce novels as superb as this. To portray such calamity so entertainingly is to surmount it. Dickens, too, presents scenes of human wretchedness (Dotheboys Hall in *Nicholas Nickleby*, for example, or Fagin's squalid den) with a comic verve and brio which transcend the misery they depict. Even so, if Sterne advocates mirth as a whole way of life, it is mostly as a prophylactic against the human shambles he finds around him. Matthew Bevis suggests that the very neatness of jokes compensates for the messiness of human mortality.[40]

The English have always had an affection for wayward, nonconformist types, men and women who like Dickens's eccentrics acknowledge no law but their own. Such types are caricatures of the free-born Englishman. People who stick a ferret down their trousers or ride to work on a baby rhino might well find themselves honoured by Buckingham Palace. This is doubtless one reason why the English love a lord, since aristocrats are natural anarchists. Those who set the rules see no reason to be bound by them. They combine the glamour of rank with the effrontery of not giving a damn. Absolute power is a kind of libertine which brooks no restraint. While the middle classes cling timorously to the social forms, the upper classes proclaim their privilege by kicking casually over the traces. As such, they have something in common with the criminal, who falls outside the law that they themselves are set above. If the criminal detests the police, the gentleman disdains them. When Brian Howard, one of the louche Evelyn Waugh set, was caught in an after-hours drinking club and asked by a police officer for his name and address, he is reputed to have replied 'My name is Brian Howard, I live in Berkeley Square, and you, Inspector, I suppose, come from some dreary little suburb.'

There is, then, a secret affinity between high and low, as there is between Lear and his Fool. As folklore attests, kings and beggars are easily reversible roles. The landowner has a stronger bond with the poacher than he has with his petty-bourgeois gamekeeper. Those who have nothing to lose may be as dangerous in their own way as those who lord it over them. It is this devil-may-careness we relish in Falstaff and Sir Toby Belch, whose roguery is spiced by the fact that they are knights of the realm. If they can knock around with the lower orders, it is because hierarchy means little to those perched at the apex of it. It is the lower-middle-class Malvolios of this world who have a jealous eye to social distinctions. When Belch declares that 'I'll confine myself no finer than I am', he speaks as an English libertarian, striking a sympathetic chord in all those curmudgeonly types who thwart the government's plans for a new airport by stubbornly clinging to their two acres of land. The liberty of the free-born Englishman lies not in a life of vigorous enterprise or ambitious schemes of self-development but in the freedom to be himself. It is the liberty of being left alone – not so that one can pursue some prodigious goal unconstrained, but so that one can potter aimlessly around one's garden or collect plaster statues of Lord Nelson. The English go to extraordinary lengths to avoid one another, or to pretend that their fellow country people are not actually there. Their celebrated reserve is less a hostility to their fellow citizens than a dogged determination to let them be. Once they are admitted to their inner sanctum, they can be loquacious enough.

The tradition of the reckless, profligate aristocrat is consummated in the career of Byron, in whom political dissent, sexual adventurism and a reputation for villainy are hard to distinguish. The blue-blooded Shelley is another such patrician rebel. In the wake of Friedrich Nietzsche, a new kind of spiritual aristocrat is born, of which Wilde and Yeats, both scions of the Anglo-Irish Ascendancy, are exemplary. The social class they sprang from in Ireland was a notoriously swashbuckling crew, profligate, spook-ridden, hard-drinking and extravagantly self-destructive. Seized by a self-vaunting swagger which the less admirable side of Yeats found deeply appealing, they could be eccentric to the point of insanity. The Gothic novelist and clergyman Charles Maturin had to be forbidden by his bishop from ceaseless frenetic dancing, while one nineteenth-century archbishop of Dublin could occasionally be spotted swinging from chains and smoking a pipe in front of his episcopal palace. John Pentland Mahaffy, Oscar Wilde's tutor at Dublin's Trinity College, once crawled into a room full of clergymen wearing only a tiger-skin rug. The wild old wicked man, as Yeats occasionally liked to see himself, would link arms with a bunch of crazed, colourful peasants in joint opposition to the monochrome world of the merchant and the clerk. Social conventions were for shop-keepers and the petty-bourgeois British. In the case of Wilde, English fop and feckless Irishman join forces against a leaden middle-class moralism.

When Charlotte Brontë names Jane Eyre's would-be seducer Rochester, after a notoriously dissolute seventeenth-century rake, it is this lineage of high-class ruffians that she has in mind. Her hero belongs to that pantheon of Satanic literary characters who are beguiling not despite their wicked-ness but because of it. The Rochester of *Jane Eyre* is finally redeemed by the love of a virtuous woman, but in his novel *Clarissa* Samuel Richardson extends no such mercy to his dastardly Lovelace, and the nobility of the Gothic novel are on the whole more predatory than enticing. Like sexuality itself, the upper classes are both attractive and alarming. One enjoys their cavalier attitude, but not the arrogance that lies at its root.

A major weapon in the campaign against middle-class gravitas is wit, a form of spontaneous humour you don't have to work for, and thus an appropriate comic mode for upper-class layabouts. There are, to be sure, other forms of wit as well, but this vein of it is particularly prominent in English culture. Wit can be both polished and brutal, thus blending the stylishness of the gentleman with his imperiousness. It can represent a suave vein of violence, as one sublimates one's aversion to others into wordplay and intellectual dexterity. As such, it is a convenient discursive mode for an ambitious outsider like Oscar Wilde, eager to impress the insiders with his virtuosity while giving vent to his animus against them in socially acceptable form. One dominates others by the superior force of personality, not by any blunter tactic. The verbal felicity of a witticism may reflect an acumen on the part of the speaker of which the victim himself would be incapable. No English fox hunter would have been capable of describing his sporting activity as Wilde did ('the unspeakable in pursuit of the uneatable').

If witticisms can be sour or stinging, they can also sweeten the pill of such hostility by the shapeliness of their form. Wit is a vein of humour which disrupts conventional expectations, deviating mischievously from the predictable; but it does so for the most part lightly and casually, without the rancour of the political militant or the heavy-handedness of the bourgeois. The aristocrat may flaunt his freedom from social norms, but he is not prepared to see them come clattering down, along with the foundations of his own privilege. Wit can be a form of frivolity, but one that redeems itself from mere vacuity by its agility of mind. In converting the serious into the sportive, it demonstrates the imperturbability of the English gentleman, whom nothing can truly unsettle. One contemplates the world as an aesthetic phenomenon, blithely, serenely, from a certain privileged distance, knowing that one is immune to misfortune and unburdened by the weight of either business or labour. Gags may be snappy or punchy, but the witticism at its finest retains a certain laid-back languor. The drawl and wordplay of a witticism can reflect a more general form of leisure. Indeed, the English nobility is traditionally so indolent that it can't even be bothered to pronounce its consonants, a tedious business it delegates to the industrious middle classes. Hence huntin', shootin' and fishin'.

Wit has a point, which is why it is sometimes compared to the thrust of a rapier. It is rapier-like in its swift, shapely, streamlined, agile, flashing, glancing, dazzling, dexterous, pointed, clashing, flamboyant aspects, but also because it can stab and wound. One commentator sees it as sadistic at heart: 'sharp, quick, alert, cold, aggressive, and hostile'.[41] Like a play of wit, fencing combines poise and elegance with a highly stylised form of aggression, being at once dexterous and potentially deadly. You can use a flash of wit to thrust but also to parry, fending off an insult with a show of insouciance. As well as making a point, this form of comedy also allows the gentleman to put his personality on public show, as a swordsman demonstrates his prowess, and thus (given that he does no work) to display one of his few precious achievements. It is himself he exhibits, not his commodities or the fruit of his exertions. He has no exertions. Wilde's finest work of art was his life, which he sculpted into shape with all the scrupulous devotion of a Michelangelo fashioning a David. The gag, by contrast, is a more impersonal comic mode, and so can circulate like a coin from hand to hand, whereas some of the finest shafts of wit bear the personal imprint of their author. They are more to be quoted than repeated.

A witticism can appear natural in the sense of apposite, spot-on, the kind of remark which once uttered might strike one as both arresting and self-evident. It is the sort of comment that one later dearly wishes one had come up with. (The French have a name for this form of regret: *l'esprit d'escalier*, or the spirit of the staircase, meaning the riposte one thinks up on the way out of the room in which one should have made it.) It is this pertinence that Alexander Pope has in mind when he writes in his *Essay on Criticism* of wit as 'Something whose truth convinc'd at sight we find, / That gives us back the image of our mind'. Yet the apparent spontaneity and off-the-cuffness of wit, the way its accuracy seems effortlessly to compel assent, belies the craft invested in it. In Pope's view, wit is Nature perfected by art. No doubt it is this artifice we admire most of all, in the spirit of Susan Sontag's definition of camp as a love of the playful, artificial, flamboyant and hyperbolic.[42] Camp in Sontag's view elevates style over content and irony over tragedy. If it reflects a comic vision, it is because it sees everything in quotation marks. It is deviant, perverse, parodic, theatrical and idiosyncratic. Like wit, it is the enemy of sentiment and empathy. The hard-boiled quality of a witticism stands at the opposite end of the comic scale from the tear and the twinkle.

There is a sense in which wit can be less a type of humour than a way of life. A wit is one who is habitually witty, whereas gags or wisecracks are sporadic affairs, brief vacations from reality. Jokes are events, whereas wit may signify a general disposition. A joke irrupts momentarily out of an everyday existence of which wit may form a seamless part. Jokes are quite often pieces of fiction, and as such mark a contrast with the workaday world, whereas witticisms, generally speaking, are not. The wit or dandy aestheticises his life along with his language, lending it the point and polish of a classical tag, and as such is never entirely off-duty. He can never be heard to ask for the salt without couching his request in epigrammatic form. Wit of this kind is a general posture towards reality, the permanent mild amusement of one who is somewhat dissociated from the world and disinclined to have his composure ruffled by acknowledging its more rebarbative aspects. In his treatise on oratory, Cicero distinguishes between barbed one-liners and witty or ironic tales in which the humour is more diffuse, woven as it is into a whole way of seeing.

Andrew Stott argues that wit 'recognises the role of chance in the production of meanings',[43] but it is not in general a form of humour hospitable to contingencies or loose ends. It is too finely wrought for that. If brevity is the soul of it, as we are informed by a Shakespearian character to whom both wit and brevity are profoundly alien, it is partly because pithiness and economy are forms of elegance, but also because the gentleman's horror of boring others inspires him to such concision, in contrast to the laborious long-windedness of the petty bourgeoisie. We speak of a 'shaft' of wit, like a spear or arrow which flies swiftly and unerringly to its target. The *Oxford English Dictionary* also defines 'shaft' as a bolt of lightning or ray of light, which captures the suddenness of wit along with its capacity to illuminate. To shaft, as well as being slang for having sex, is also to worst or discomfit, so that you can be shafted by a shaft of wit. A witticism is a self-conscious verbal performance, but it is one that minimises its own medium, compacting its words into the slimmest possible space in an awareness that the slightest surplus of signification might prove fatal to its success. As with poetry, every verbal unit must pull its weight, and the cadence, rhythm and resonance of a piece of wit may be vital to its impact. The tighter the organisation, the more a verbal slide, ambiguity, conceptual shift or trifling dislocation of syntax registers its effect. The compactness of a witticism throws into relief any sudden shift of perspective or inversion of meaning. As far as the former goes, one thinks of the Dublin wit Seán Mac Réamoinn's comment that he felt rather like the Irish census: broken down by age, sex and religion. When it comes to inversions of meaning, Mac Réamoinn once rang a change on the cliché that inside every fat man there's a slim man struggling to get out by remarking that outside every slim man there's a fat man struggling to get in.

No doubt this condensation is why the faculty of wit has sometimes been thought to reflect the unmediated, intuitive knowledge of the Almighty himself, who is able to dispense with the cumbersome business of discursive communication. Matthew Bevis remarks that a joke always says what it says in too few words,[44] and of no brand of humour is this truer than wit. By streamlining one's material, one allows the recipient to economise on his or her reception of it, and this labour-saving is part of the witticism's comic force. We are gratified by the lapidary form as well as by the revelatory content. More than with almost any other form of humour, much of our delight lies in the artistry of the utterance, which is one reason why witticisms do not need to be particularly funny to be entertaining. In an interplay of freedom and constraint, language is allowed to frolic for a moment, but in strictly regulated style.

Pope famously defines wit as 'What oft was thought but ne'er so well exprest'; but this is to confine it to the signifier alone, which does it less than justice. As a stout neo-classicist, Pope is bound to take this line because in his view there cannot strictly speaking be any new truth. Innovation is mostly errant and fanciful. Wit can improve on Nature, as a landscape gardener may bring out the inherent beauties of a terrain, but it cannot produce any novel insight. Instead, it reminds us in memorably incisive terms of what we know already. The Romantic Hazlitt, for whom invention and originality are virtues, is surely nearer the mark when he describes wit as 'a nimble sagacity of apprehension, a special felicity of invention, a vivacity of spirit'.[45] As with metaphor, there can be a cognitive as well as ludic aspect to it. As with certain complex jokes, this may involve the sudden intellectual pleasure of getting the point, rather like the mild sense of elation involved in solving a puzzle. An element of surprise or moment of illumination is generally central to the practice. As George Santayana observes in *The Sense of Beauty*, it is a question of 'unexpected justness'. 'Our laughter when we get a joke,' comments Matthew Bevis, 'announces a triumph: the salvaging of cognitive prowess from momentary weakness.'[46] One might claim that wit in particular represents a minor victory of mind over matter – of a supple creative intelligence over the intractability of the world. Certainly this was Wilde's own belief. 'When man acts, he is a puppet,' remarks Gilbert in Wilde's *The Critic as Artist*. 'When he describes, he is a poet.' Action is blind, flawed, ignorant and rigorously determined, mired in the contingencies of a mindlessly repetitive Nature. Art or wit, by contrast, represent a momentary leap out of the realm of necessity into the kingdom of freedom. They offer some compensation for the *longueurs* of everyday existence, not least in the harsh conditions of England's oldest colony.

The pleasures of wit, then, are complex ones. We delight simultaneously in the artistry of the form, the dexterity of the performance, the labour-saving economy of the succinct language, the free play of mind, the inversions, subversions, surprises and dislocations of the content, the intellectual satisfaction of 'getting' it and the display of personality it involves, while the malice, insolence or disdain which may lurk behind a witticism allows us a certain vicarious release. We also take sadistic pleasure in seeing the target of wit momentarily discomfited. If the form of wit we have examined is distinctively patrician, however, it is worth recalling that there are plebeian modes of humour, too, which we shall now go on to investigate.

5

THE POLITICS OF HUMOUR

Perhaps the single most contradictory political phenomenon of the modern world is nationalism, which ranges from the Nazi death camps to a principled resistance to imperial power. In terms of sheer political ambiguity, however, humour runs it fairly close. If it can censure, debunk and transform, it can also dissolve essential social conflicts in an explosion of mirth. Mutual laughter can be a form of mutual disarming, as the physical dissolution of the laughing body signals that it is incapable of inflicting harm. 'He who laughs cannot bite,' observes Norbert Elias.[1] As such, it can furnish us with a utopian image of a peaceable domain to come. 'Perhaps, even if nothing else today has any future,' writes Friedrich Nietzsche, 'our laughter has a future.'[2] Yet the helpless, uncoordinated body is hardly in a state to construct that social order. In this sense, comedy represents no threat to a sovereign power.

Indeed, such powers have a vested interest in the good humour of the populace. A dispirited nation may prove to be a disaffected one. Yet rulers also require the common people to be diligent and dutiful, to exercise self-discipline and take their jobs seriously, and all this may well be jeopardised by a wave of gloriously irresponsible euphoria.

Like art, humour can estrange and relativise the norms by which we live, but it can also reinforce them. In fact, it can do so precisely by estranging them. To inspect one's everyday behaviour through alien eyes is not necessarily to alter it. On the contrary, it might yield us a keener sense of its legitimacy. In typically liberal spirit, Jonathan Miller sees humour as a free play of the mind which loosens up our routine conceptual categories, relaxes their despotism and prevents us from becoming their slaves. We can now envisage different forms of classification, redesigning our everyday frames of reference.[3] But there is no reason to believe that all this will inevitably result in a more enlightened state of mind. Why should we assume that all of our current categories are in need of reconstruction? Is a belief in gender equality a conceptual hindrance we need to break free from? And why should Miller's liberalism not itself be subjected to such a critique? The anthropologist Mary Douglas regards all jokes as subversive since they expose the essential arbitrariness of social meanings. 'A joke,' she writes, 'symbolises levelling, dissolution and renewal.'[4] In a classic earlier study, *Purity and Danger*, Douglas runs a similar argument about dirt, seen as unclassifiable, out-of-place material which marks the limits of our social constructions, a case which lends a new meaning to the term 'dirty joke'. It is hard, however, to brand Jay Leno or Graham Norton as subversives.

In contrary spirit, Susan Purdie argues in an attractively ambitious study that jokes transgress authority only to end up reinstating it, though this overlooks the fact that not all forms of authority are oppressive.[5] There is the authority of veteran dissidents as well as of those who hound them, of civil rights movements as well as of despotic governments. Noël Carroll also holds that in alerting us to certain social norms, humour helps to reinforce them.[6] The rather more tedious truth, however, is that sometimes it does and sometimes it doesn't. In any case, there are social norms that urgently need reinforcing. It is normative in British society that working people have the right under certain conditions to withdraw their labour. Norms are not always sinisterly coercive devices. To see humour as always and everywhere a reinforcement of power is too functionalist a standpoint, overlooking its manifest contradictions.

Alenka Zupančič writes with rash generality of how comedy 'sustains the very oppression of the given order or situation, because it makes it bearable and induces the illusion of an effective interior freedom'.[7] Konrad Lorenz also treats the comic as essentially conservative, remarking that 'laughter forms a bond and simultaneously draws a line'.[8] He means that the solidarity humour breeds is inseparable from a sense of one's difference from others, and may thus breed a certain antagonism towards them. In this sense, it is both bond and weapon.[9] Lorenz also thinks in Whiggish style that humour has progressed historically – that we are funnier now than we were in antiquity, and that contemporary humour is in general subtler and more searching than that of our ancestors. Not much before Dickens, he comments curiously, is likely to raise a laugh. He also maintains that the human being is a 'self-ridiculing' animal, though this may be truer of English liberals than of US Republicans.

If the solidarity humour generates is indeed dependent on exclusion and antagonism, then humour is at odds with the cosmic sense of the comic, which embraces the whole of reality in its tolerant, benevolent style. Noël Carroll believes that where there is an Us there is also typically a Them, but Francis Hutcheson, for one, would have demurred. The utopia of which laughter is a foretaste has no fixed bounds. The audiences of comedy shows do not feel bathed in a tide of collective euphoria only because they have some other bunch of men and women to feel ill-disposed towards. Humour may be conflictive or communitarian, denigratory or celebratory, but the two need not be sides of the same coin. There is a problem for the political left, even so, in reconciling humour as utopia with humour as critique; and to cast light on this and other questions, we may turn now to Trevor Griffiths's classic drama *Comedians*.

In a school classroom in Manchester, a bunch of aspiring amateur comics are being put through their paces by the once renowned but now retired comedian Eddie Waters, a man who has thought long and deep about the nature of humour. His students include Ged Murray, a milkman, his brother Phil, an insurance agent, Sammy Samuels, a Mancunian Jew who runs a third-rate night club, George McBrain, a Northern Irish docker, Mick Connor, an Irish labourer, and Gethin Price, who drives a van for British Rail. Trapped in dead-end jobs, all six men see success as professional comedians as the only route out of them. They are shortly to be auditioned for such careers by Bert Challenor, a London-based show-business entrepreneur and long-time adversary of Waters. A slick, cynical operator with a thin veneer of charm, Challenor is on the hunt for comedians who keep it simple, avoid deep thought, give the public what they want and offer them a momentary refuge from their everyday lives. 'We're not missionaries,' he warns Waters's students, 'we're suppliers of laughter.' Comedy in his view is a commodity sold to yobbos who neither want to learn nor are capable of doing so, and its practitioners need to sell their wares dear rather than give them away. 'All audiences are thick,' Challenor declares, 'but it's a bad comedian who lets 'em know it.' If they can be led, he insists, it is only in the direction they wish to go.

Eddie Waters's philosophy of humour is somewhat less primitive. At one point in the proceedings, he asks his pupils to think of some disconcerting experience in their lives – 'anything, any little thing, that means something to you, maybe something that embarrasses you or haunts you or still makes you frightened, something you still can't deal with maybe, all right?' Ged Murray thinks back to a chilling moment in a maternity ward when he suddenly feared that his newborn child might be disabled, then sees with relief that 'he were bloody perfect'. Gethin Price recalls an occasion on which he thumped a woman teacher for calling him a guttersnipe, and was packed off to a psychiatrist for his pains. The others preserve an uneasy silence, unable to rise to Waters's challenge. What flummoxes them is not only the invitation to show fear or frailty in the presence of their hard-boiled colleagues, but the fact that Waters has instructed them to make their accounts funny.

This is not humour as disavowal. The point is not to disown the pain, but to allow it to resonate through one's discourse, dredging the comedy up from a depth of affliction or anxiety, rage or humiliation so as to invest it with the authority of that experience. In articulating the unspeakable, in a sense more exacting than coming up with insults or obscenities, it must transcend the trauma in question without simply negating it, an exercise that demands both courage and truthfulness. As a way of liberating others into similar acts of confession, such dark humour is also a form of communication and comradeship. Most of Waters's gang put themselves on hold as individuals while cracking jokes, pattering glibly off the top of their heads, while Gethin Price, as we shall see in a moment, gives all-too-raw vent to his personal hang-ups. What Waters requires, by contrast with both strategies, is an ugly or fearful truth which has been transmuted into art – shaped, distanced and surmounted by the comic spirit while retaining all of its formidable force.

The opposite of tackling one's pain while acknowledging one's weakness is to inflict pain on others by deriding their alleged defects, which is what comic abuse amounts to. Genuinely to find one's own discomfiture funny demands a degree of self-insight and self-mastery, whereas to jeer at others is among other things a way of disavowing one's own anxieties. Learning to confront one's own tribulations without sentimentality or self-indulgence is thus an object lesson in learning to respond to the sufferings of others. 'Do we fear . . . other people . . . so much,' Waters inquires, 'that we must mark their pain with laughter, our own with tears?' 'A real comedian – that's a daring man,' he comments.

> He *dares* to see what his listeners shy away from, fear to express. And what he sees is a sort of truth, about people, about their situation, about what hurts or terrifies them,

about what's hard, above all, about what they *want*. A joke releases the tension, says the unsayable, any joke pretty well. But a true joke, a comedian's joke, has to do more than release tension, it has to *liberate* the will and the desire, it has to change the situation.

Humour for Waters is risk, candour, danger, courage, exposure, intervention. If it is fiction, it also has the abrasive truthfulness of great art.

Waters's comment is more ambiguous than he seems to recognise. Genuine comedians give voice to what others shy away from, perceiving the truth about what hurts or terrifies them. Yet this could also be claimed of racist and sexist humour, which in giving tongue to the ethnic and sexual anxieties of the audience seeks to say the conventionally unsayable. The comic who calls women slags or blacks coons also articulates what his hearers might generally want but evade and fear to express, and in doing so he, too, releases tension. Waters's remarks seem not fully to register this disquieting parallel, but as if sensing it, and anxious to mark the distinction between this degenerate brand of comedy and truly emancipatory humour, he insists that a real joke has to liberate and transform as well as release.

When Gethin Price comes up with an inventive but repellently sexist limerick, Waters responds with the following terrifying diatribe:

I've never liked the Irish, you know . . . Big, thick, stupid heads, large cabbage ears, hairy nostrils, daft eyes, fat, flapping hands, stinking of soil and Guinness. The niggers of Europe. Huge, uncontrollable wangers, spawning their degenerate kind wherever they're allowed to settle. I'd stop them settling here if I had my way. Send 'em back to the primordial bog they came from. Potato heads . . .

They have this *greasy* quality, do Jews. Stick to their own. Grafters. Fixers. Money. Always money. Say Jew, say gold. Moneylenders, pawnbrokers, usurers. They have the nose for it, you might say. Hitler put it more bluntly: 'If we do not take steps to maintain the purity of blood, the Jew will destroy civilization by poisoning us all.' The effluent of history. Scarcely human. Grubs . . .

Workers. Dirty. Unschooled. Shifty. Grabbing all they can get. Putting coal in the bath. Chips with everything. Chips and beer. Trade Unions dedicated to maximizing wages and minimizing work. Strikes for the idle. Their greed. And their bottomless stupidity. Like children, unfit to look after themselves. Breeding like rabbits, sex-mad. And their mean vicious womenfolk, driving them on. Animals, to be fed slops and fastened up at night.

Waters's foul rant represents a savage assault on the audience as well as on his bemused students, who are more accustomed to hearing this kind of talk from their own mouths rather than from his. One can easily imagine theatres today where it would be cut.

On learning that Challenor, who holds their futures in the palm of his hand, is the kind of bigot who appreciates a spot of racist and sexist vitriol from his entertainers, most of Waters's pupils unceremoniously ditch what he has taught them and revert to their customary combination of smut and racist invective. The Irish labourer Mick Connor, who comes up with a string of low-grade but relatively innocuous wise-cracks, marks an exception, but Sammy Samuels provides an ugly object lesson in the superiority theory:

There's this West Indian tries to get a labouring job on a building site. Foreman says, No chance, I know you lot. I give one of you a job, you turn up the next day with a gang of your friends. He begs and pleads and finally he gets the job. Next day he turns up with a pigmy. (*Indicating.*) Pigmy. Down there. The foreman said, What did I tell you, no friends! He says, That's not my friend, that's my lunch. What do you think of this Women's Lib, then? Burnt your bras have you? Did you, sir, how interesting. I burnt the wife's. She went bloody mad, she was still in it. I'm in a pub downtown and this liberated woman person collars me, she says, You're a brutal, loud-mouthed, sadistic, irrational, sexist, male chauvinist pig. I said, I suppose a quick screw is out of the question?

145

George McBrain cravenly follows suit:

> I was in bed with the wife last Thursday. The wife lay there, very quiet, smoking her pipe. I leaned across and I said, Do you fancy anything, heart? And she said, Yes, I fancy an African about six-foot-three with a big fat . . . cheque book. (*To audience.*) Don't get ahead of yourselves! Naughty! I said, Yeah? And what do you reckon he'd make of that great fat idle bum of yours? And she said, what makes you think we'd be talking about you? Doesn't say a lot, my wife. Talks all the time but doesn't say a lot.

Ged and Phil Murray stage a double act, with Ged struggling to stay true to his teacher's counsel while Phil, with an uneasy eye on Challenor, insists on telling a joke about a Pakistani up on a rape charge. Torn down the middle between two antithetical views of humour, the act falls embarrassingly apart.

There is, however, no easy opposition between humour as transformation and humour as vilification. There is much to be said for abuse, whatever today's conventional wisdom may hold. The school caretaker enters at the end of the play to wipe a number of obscene words from the classroom blackboard, muttering 'The dirty buggers' as he does so, but his objection to cursing is merely prudish. He fails to see that foul language can also serve a function. When Challenor selects the crudest of Waters's men for potential stardom, Waters tells him that he is as full of shit as a large intestine, an insult that is entirely well earned. Like most of his colleagues, Gethin Price has also altered his act on hearing of Challenor's proclivities, but in order to confront him, not to win his approval. Price, a mixture of Fool, satirist, parodist, mime artist, dissident and shape-shifter, enters with his face whitened, dressed like a cross between a clown and a yob, and performs a chilling, weirdly menacing act that involves mocking and berating a couple of dummies, one male and one female, decked out as faintly arrogant upper-middle-class types in evening dress. He blows smoke in the man's face, misses his head by inches with a kung fu thrust and insults his girlfriend. Pinning a flower between the woman's breasts, he causes a dark red bloodstain to appear on her dress. He ends his act by playing 'The Red Flag' on a minuscule violin. Some people, he comments, would call his tongue-lashing envy, but he denies the charge: it's hate.

Challenor rightly describes Price's eerie, outlandishly avant-garde performance as 'aggressively unfunny', as opposed to the routines of the other comics, which are both aggressive and unfunny. What Price has done is preserve the patter and stylish performance of a comedy act while evacuating it of its conventional content. In a powerful showdown between him and Waters – their relationship is a subtly nuanced blend of friendship, rivalry, dissent and discipleship – Waters concedes that his student was technically brilliant but denounces his act as 'terrifying'. 'No compassion, no truth,' he tells him. 'You threw it all out, Gethin. Love, care, concern, call it what you like, you junked it over the side.' Price himself maintains that when it comes to the class system, love and compassion would only serve to mystify the unpalatable truth. If his act is offensive, it is because what it represents is offensive, and it is hypocritical to complain about the former while saying nothing of the latter. The case sails uncomfortably close to the so-called mimetic fallacy – the claim, for example, that one's novel was meant to be excruciatingly boring because of the excruciatingly boring situations it portrays. Price's outrageous charade is deliberately stylised, deadened and dehumanised in order to scandalise what Bertolt Brecht once called 'the scum who want the cockles of their hearts warmed'. In Price's militant view, that kind of sentiment, epitomised by the saccharine little ditty with which the Murray brothers conclude their disastrous double act ('He watches over me / When things get tough / He pulls the strings / That wipe the tears away on my cuff') is simply the icing on the cake of exploitation, the emotional window-dressing of a heartless social order. To Waters's charge that he has ditched the truth, Price retorts angrily that the truth is ugly and that Waters, who knew this well enough as a struggling young comic, may now have forgotten the fact:

THE POLITICS OF HUMOUR

Nobody hit harder than Eddie Waters, that's what they say. Because you were still in touch with what made you . . . hunger, diphtheria, filth, unemployment, penny clubs, means tests, bed bugs, head lice . . . Was all *that* truth beautiful? . . . Truth was a fist you hit with . . . We're still caged, exploited, prodded and pulled at, milked, fattened, slaughtered, cut up, fed out. We still don't belong to ourselves. Nothing's changed. You've just forgotten, that's all.

Throughout the three months of their comedy class, he charges, Waters has never said a single funny thing. It is indeed hard to credit that this grim-faced, heavily moralistic, internally broken man once ranked among the finest of British comedians. Perhaps, Price remarks sourly, he has lost his hate.

It is not this, however, that accounts for Waters's decline. Driven on to the back foot by his pupil's onslaught, which has more than a touch of the rebellious son's disillusionment with the failed father, he is forced to reach into his own most harrowing recollections in order to justify himself. He, too, must confront his ghosts, as he has urged his students to do. He tells Price of a visit he once made to a former Nazi concentration camp in Germany, and how at the very moment of being repelled by what he saw, he got an erection. It was then he discovered that there were no jokes left. Just as Theodor Adorno declared that all poetry after Auschwitz is garbage, so

Waters, hearing a joke about a Jew at a concert on the evening of his visit to the death camp, ceased to laugh. 'We've gotta get deeper than hate,' he tells Price. 'Hate's no help.' Price takes up a superior stance to the system he satirises, whereas Waters's sexual arousal suggests that he is somehow complicit with it, and thus needs to undo that monstrosity in himself as well.

If hate is no help, however, what about hatred of injustice? If comedy is to turn its back on abhorrence and antagonism, how is it to confront the forces that fashioned the so-called Final Solution in the first place? Is not a properly rancorous humour an indispensable weapon in the armoury of the political satirist – of those artists in the Weimar Republic, for example, who travestied and lampooned Hitler on his trek to power? Yet how is such pugnacity not to be tainted with the very inhumanity it exists to decry? It is the problem posed by the greatest of Weimar literary artists, Bertolt Brecht, in his poem 'To Those Born Later':

> For we went, changing countries more often than our shoes
> Through the wars of the classes, despairing
> When there was injustice only, and no rebellion.
>
> And yet we know:
> Hatred, even of meanness
> Makes you ugly.
> Anger, even at injustice

Makes your voice hoarse. Oh, we
Who wanted to prepare the land for friendliness
Could not ourselves be friendly.

You, however, when the time comes
When mankind is a helper unto mankind
Think on us
With forbearance.

The values involved in building a just society may run counter to the virtues which are meant to flourish there. Friendship demands enmity, peace requires conflict and faith entails scepticism. In this sense, those who devote their lives to emancipatory politics are by no means the most accurate images of what they hope to create. Even hatred of injustice can makes the voice hoarse; and any form of hate can acquire a deadly momentum of its own, one which becomes autonomous of its political goal.

The question, then, is how friendship and enmity are to be combined in the same comic mode. As Raymond Williams remarks in the Conclusion to *Culture and Society 1780–1950* of 1958, one of the icons of the labour movement must necessarily be a closed fist, but the closing must not be such that the fingers cannot open to shape a new social reality. It is not an issue that particularly troubles Gethin Price, a man who is perhaps anyway as much a dissident individualist as a socialist militant. His view, as we have seen, is that if the truth is unlovely, then so must its portrayal be. Waters refuses this case: in his view, comedy exists to dredge such intransigent stuff to light and in doing so come to terms with it, but to do so *as comedy*. 'Most comics,' he tells his pupils, '*feed* prejudice and fear and blinkered vision, but the best ones, the best ones . . . illuminate them, make them clearer to see, easier to cope with.' Comedy establishes a cognitive distance from its object, and in doing so knows it as it cannot know itself. It must shape and surmount its materials, not simply reflect them. Its form is in this sense askew to its content. Yet Waters's account of what happened to him in the concentration camp strikes a more sombre note. If the truth is terrible, then perhaps humour of any kind is simply a blasphemy. This, as it happens, overlooks the fact that some of the inmates of the concentration camps told jokes themselves in a struggle to preserve their sanity. Samuels, McBrain and Phil Murray, whose humour is hideous precisely because it betrays the truth, represent a third position.

There is a parallel between Price's sadistic charade and Waters's experience in the camp. From a Freudian viewpoint, the latter's erotic arousal is a case of *jouissance*, or obscene enjoyment, as the ego reaps pleasure from the spectacle of death, and thus from the prospect of its own demise. *Eros* and *Thanatos* are in cahoots. There is something perversely exhilarating about sheer nothingness, a state in which the bruised, battered ego can no longer suffer harm. To be relieved of one's humanity was the fate of those who died in the camps, but it can also be a momentary release from anxiety and affliction. What Waters's guilt prevents him from perceiving is that it is human to desire the inhuman. Price has no such qualms. On the contrary, it is precisely the dehumanised nature of his performance that enthrals him. 'It was all ice out there tonight,' he tells Waters. 'I loved it. I felt . . . expressed.' Theoretically speaking, his act is a combination of superiority and release. He is a devotee of the great clown Grock, whose hardness and truthfulness he finds appealing – 'Not like Chaplin, all coy and covered with kids.' Price's bizarre panto-mime is aimed at destroying the sentimental idealism that is the acceptable face of political inhumanity, including that of the Nazi regime; but it cannot do so without colluding to some extent with that inhumanity. In its own minor key, it is as much an example of living death as Buchenwald, even if it is against such horrors that it is aimed.

In the end, then, neither Waters nor Price can reconcile truth and comedy. They are as incapable of doing so as Samuels and McBrain, if for quite different reasons. Truth has struck Waters's humour dumb, while Price's satire is pure steel. How can one be funny and truthful at the same time in inhuman conditions? In any case, is Waters right to view humour purely as a tool of political change? There is no doubt that this can be one of its functions, but his approach to comedy is surely too instrumentalist. It is of a piece with his didacticism, a flaw that the play seems uneasily aware of without explicitly criticising. The nearest it sails to such scrutiny is a hilarious moment in which Price, a superb mimic, sends up his sermonising teacher behind his back. What of the utopian function of comedy as friendship and festivity, sheer pointless delight in sharing and solidarity, an anticipation of an age of peace and kindliness rather than a strategy for bringing it to birth? If humour for the likes of Samuels and McBrain is a blunt instrument of their prejudices, isn't Waters reproducing this utilitarian logic in his own more enlightened fashion? 'We work *through* laughter,' he tells the others, 'not *for* it. If all you're about is raising a laugh, OK, get on with it, good luck to you, but don't waste my time.' 'Comedy is medicine,' he remarks a little later. 'Not coloured sweeties to rot [an audience's] teeth with.' It is a puritanical case that the play leaves curiously unchallenged. McBrain remarks with typical thick-headedness that 'A comic's a comic's a comic.' This isn't true, as the play shows. But it is sometimes true that a joke is a joke is a joke.

Despite this, *Comedians* does indeed end on a quasi-utopian note. An Asian, Mr Patel, who has wandered into the school in search of an evening class, encounters Waters and volunteers to tell him a joke from his own country, one that involves the idea of slaughtering sacred cows. It is a vein of humour congenial to both Waters and Price, though it is delivered with an innocent verve which the former has lost, and which the latter might well find politically suspect. In an empty school classroom which has just borne witness to comedy as insult, bigotry, acrimony, commodity, dissent, ferocious rivalry, unscrupulous self-promotion and icing the cake of inhumanity, humour becomes for a precious moment a medium of interracial friendship, as Waters invites Mr Patel to join his next class.

Comedians does not seek to resolve the conflicts it portrays so finely. Providing solutions is the task of policy makers, not dramatists. Yet there is in fact a way of combining humour as critique with humour as utopia, and its name is carnival. If the clubs and coffee houses of Hutcheson and Steele constitute a bourgeois public sphere, one in which rank is suspended for a free and equal exchange between gentlemen, carnival, in which much the same suspension of rank occurs, figures in some ways as its plebeian counterpart. As a counter-culture which is simultaneously real and ideal, actual yet future-oriented, it represents a utopian domain of freedom, community, equality and superabundance, in which all status, norms, privileges and prohibitions are temporarily put on hold. In their place, a free, frank idiom of the streets and marketplaces is unleashed, diminishing the distance between individuals and liberating them from the requirements of decency and etiquette. The barriers of caste, profession, property and age are overturned. Folly becomes a form of festive wisdom in this cornucopian world. Truth and authority are remoulded into a Mardi Gras dummy, a comic monster that the crowd rends to pieces in the marketplace rather more jubilantly than Gethin Price mauls his tailor's models. Laughter becomes a new style of communication, the material sign of a transformed set of social relations. There is 'the potentiality of a friendly world, of the golden age, of carnival truth. Man returns to himself.'[10]

Yet the discourse of carnival is double-edged. If it is in search of a transfigured world of liberty, fellowship and equality, it mocks, lampoons and disfigures in order to attain it. Its critical and affirmative functions are thus at one. Popular revelry is a riotously deconstructive force, collapsing hierarchies, travestying sacred truths, deflating exalted doctrines and mischievously inverting high and low, but this disruptive activity is all in the cause of fun and friendship. We have seen that for Konrad Lorenz humour is both bond and weapon – but only in the sense that fellowship is forged through antagonism, which is not the case with carnival. This great orgy of iconoclasm is a matter of both violence and comradeship, cursing and praising, slander and festivity. It affirms and denies, buries and resurrects in a single gesture. If there are gargantuan feasts and erotic couplings, there is also an outrageous vein of obloquy, of the kind one finds often enough in Rabelais:

> May St. Anthony sear you with his erysipelatous fire . . . may Mahomet's disease whirl you in epileptic jitters . . .

may the festers, ulcers and chancres of every purulent pox
infect, scathe, mangle and rend you, entering your bumgut
as tenuously as mercuralized cow's hair . . . and may you
vanish into an abyss of brimstone and fire, like Sodom and
Gomorrah, if you do not believe implicitly what I am
about to relate in the present *Chronicles* (p. 164).

Rabelasian cursing is inexhaustibly fertile, exuberant and
inventive, as the patter of Samuels and McBrain is not. Yet
this language is Janus-faced, too, veering from calumny to
celebration. As Bakhtin remarks, carnivalesque discourse
praises while abusing and abuses while praising. It mortifies
and humiliates, but at the same time revivifies and replen-
ishes. Even at its most scabrous, such laughter retains a regen-
erative quality. It never lapses à la Price into cutting irony or
chilling sarcasm. Bakhtin speaks of 'familiar, friendly abuse'
(p. 168), in which vilification operates within a broader
context of solidarity and high spirits. Rabelasian language is
marked by both a multiplicity of meaning and a peculiarly
complex relation to its object. As Bakhtin puts it, 'Frank
mockery and praise, dethroning and exaltation, irony and
dithyramb, are here combined' (p. 142). Yet there is no question of superiority in its scoldings, not least since there are
no spectators in the sphere of carnival to condescend to its
participants. Instead, the whole world, in principle at least,
pitches in. It is humanity itself that is on stage, a stage that

is coextensive with the auditorium. 'The satirist whose laughter is negative,' Bakhtin remarks, 'places himself above the object of his mockery' (p. 12), but at carnival time the populace taunt themselves, as subjects and objects of satire in a single body.

Carnival degrades and debases, then, but in a way that is hard to distinguish from affirmation. 'To degrade,' writes Bakhtin,

> means to concern oneself with the lower stratum of the body, the life of the belly and the reproductive organs; it therefore relates to acts of defecation and copulation, conception, pregnancy, and birth. Degradation digs a bodily grave for a new birth; it has not only a destructive, negative aspect, but also a regenerative one. To degrade an object does not imply merely hurling it into the void of nonexistence, into absolute destruction, but to hurl it down to the reproductive lower stratum, the zone in which conception and a new birth take place (p. 21).

It is this ambivalently fruitful and denigratory mode to which Bakhtin gives the name of grotesque realism. 'The essence of the grotesque,' he writes, 'is precisely to present a contradictory and double-faced fullness of life. Negation and destruction (death of the old) are included as an essential phase, inseparable from affirmation, from the birth of something new and better' (p. 62). One recalls that the word comedy derives from Comus, an ancient fertility god who signifies perpetual rejuvenation.

Carnivalesque comedy is a form of vulgar materialism, one which re-roots its subjects in the earth and in doing so allows them to fructify. It signifies 'the lowering of all that is high, spiritual, ideal, abstract' (p. 19), but only so that its true value may be extracted from this mystical shell. If its ferocious demolition of abstract idealism has a smack of the death drive about it (a 'wish for death', as Bakhtin himself puts it), it is also intertwined with a 'wish for life'. One can lay waste to the world as savagely as one likes, convinced that matter, along with the great body of the populace, is imperishable, and that each act of annihilation is simply the prelude to a new birth. If the earth is a grave, it is also a womb. The immortality of the collective body is reflected in the inviolability of the individual one, as men and women are ritually beaten and buffeted but in cartoon-like fashion remain magically unscathed. Carnival is violence fictionalised, virtualised, alchemised into theatre and spectacle, and as such a jovial kind of belligerence.

In Bakhtin's view, the grotesque or carnivalesque body is unfinished, open-ended, perpetually in process. As such, it is a riposte to the timeless, absolute status of official ideologies. One such oppressive dogma, the name of which must remain unspoken, is Stalinism. It is the body's orifices in particular which seize his attention, those liminal places at which a man or woman is open to the world and where firm distinctions between inner and outer, self and reality or self and others, begin to falter:

> All these convexities and orifices have a common characteristic; it is within them that the confines between bodies and between the body and the world are overcome: there is an interchange and an interorientation ... Eating, drinking, defecation and other elimination (sweating, blowing of the nose, sneezing), as well as copulation, pregnancy, dismemberment, swallowing up by another body – all these acts are performed on the confines of the body and the outer world, or on the confines of the old and new body. In all these events the beginning and end of life are closely linked and interwoven (p. 317).

Like laughter, the body itself for Bakhtin is a mode of relationship, the fleshly focus of human exchanges and interactions. It is what binds the individual into an eternal collectivity, and as such partakes of a vicarious immortality. I die, but we do not. It is from this joyful assurance that the fearlessness of carnival, its exuberant sense of being insulated from harm, can be seen to spring. At a later point in European history, so Bakhtin argues, the individual body will be amputated from this collective to become sanitised and gentrified, its orifices closed off, its space rigorously delimited:

That which protrudes, bugles, sprouts, or branches off [when a body transgresses its limits and a new one begins] is eliminated, hidden, or moderated. ... The opaque surface and the body's 'valleys' acquire an essential meaning as the border of a closed individuality that does not merge with other bodies and with the world (p. 320).

It is the ambivalence of the flesh, then, that lies at the basis of the two-toned nature of carnivalesque discourse. The blending of praise and calumny, utopia and critique that marks the speech patterns of this saturnalia is anchored in the simultaneous decay and renewal, defecation and copulation, of the human body. 'Whenever men laugh and curse,' Bakhtin writes, 'particularly in a familiar environment, their speech is filled with bodily images. The body copulates, defecates, over-eats, and men's speech is flooded with genitals, bellies, defeca-tions, urine, diseases, noses, mouths, and dismembered parts' (p. 319). The mouth, for example, bites, tears and devours, but in doing so recharges the body, assimilating the world to itself in a utopian alliance with Nature.

The vigilant reader may have detected a certain idealising strain in Bakhtin's extravagant hymn of praise to the common folk. Carnival would seem a world that has banished tragedy. There is an acceptance of death, to be sure, but only as a spring-board to new life. Agony and affliction are not confronted as realities in themselves, in all their terror and intractability. In

161

this sense, the carnivalesque spirit is one of several modes by which death can be disavowed. It is not, as it is with Eddie Waters of *Comedians*, a question of salvaging value from a pain which remains insistent, but of converting that pain into joy. There are other reasons to be sceptical of Bakhtin's case. For one thing, we have rather less reason in our own epoch to be persuaded that our species is imperishable. For another thing, carnival may be a fictionalised form of insurrection, but it also provides a safety valve for such subversive energies. In this sense, its closest parallel today is professional sport, the abolition of which would no doubt be the shortest route to bloody revolution.

Finally, we may note that Bakhtin's censure of the medieval church overlooks the carnivalesque features of the Christian gospel. Many a commentator has observed that though Jesus weeps, he does not laugh, a reticence that might seem in line with the Book of Ecclesiastes's grim insistence that 'Sorrow is better than laughter, for by the sadness of the countenance the heart is made glad. The heart of the wise is in the house of mourning, but the heart of fools is in the house of mirth' (7:3–4). It is true that the Jesus portrayed by the New Testament is hardly remarkable for his side-splitting sense of fun, having as he did a fair amount to feel glum about. (There are, however, Gnostic documents that see Simon of Cyrene as having been crucified in Jesus's place, and describe Jesus as laughing in heaven at the sight.)[11] It will be a sign that his kingdom is imminent, however, when we see the poor being filled with good things and the rich sent empty away, a classic carnivalesque inversion. Unlike the reversals and up-endings of carnival, this will prove more than a temporary affair. Enid Welsford records that at vespers on the medieval Feast of Fools, the gospel words 'He has put down the mighty from their seat and exalted the lowly' were sung over and over again, as the prelude to a mischievous parody of the Mass.[12] Jesus and his plebeian comrades do no work, are accused of drunkenness and gluttony, roam footloose and propertyless on the margins of the conventional social order, and like the free spirits of carnival take no thought for tomorrow. As a sick joke of a Saviour (the notion of a crucified Messiah would have struck the ancient Jews as a moral obscenity), Jesus enters Jerusalem, the stronghold of Roman imperial power, on the back of a donkey, and having been deserted by his comrades will be left to face an ignominious death, one reserved by the Romans for political rebels alone. Yet the folly of the cross proves wiser than the wisdom of the philosophers. The intimidatory power of the Law is overthrown, the meek inherit the earth, the sublime becomes human flesh and blood, the most sacred truths are cast in a plain idiom intended for fishermen and small farmers, and weakness proves the only durable form of strength.

Carnivalesque bathos lies at the core of Christianity, as the awesome question of salvation comes down to the earthly, everyday business of tending the sick and feeding the hungry. Luke's gospel promises that those who weep now, meaning the afflicted and dispossessed, will laugh later – though it also reverses this reversal by warning that those who laugh now, meaning the well-heeled and self-satisfied, will weep later. The profound ease and euphoria of spirit known as divine grace manifests itself among other things in human mercy, friendship and forgiveness. In the Eucharist as in carnival, flesh and blood become a medium of communion and solidarity between human beings. Yet if the New Testament commends a laid-back life free of anxiety, in which one lives like the lilies of the field and turns one's goods over to the poor, it also portrays its protagonist as wielding a sword, one which enforces an absolute division between those who seek justice and fellowship and those who turn their backs on this ruthlessly uncompromising campaign. Like carnival, the gospel combines the joy of liberation with a certain violence and intransigence of spirit. Jesus's curses, directed at those respectable religious types who fasten extra burdens on the backs of those already sorely oppressed, are at least as terrifying as Rabelais', if not quite as entertaining. There is also a vein of *comédie noire* in Christianity. God sends his only son to save us from our plight, and how do we show our gratitude? We kill him! It is an appalling display of bad manners.

ENDNOTES

PREFACE

1. For such 'scientific' studies, see, for example, Ivatore Attardo, *Linguistic Theories of Humor* (Berlin and New York, NY, 1994) and Victor Raskin (ed.), *The Primer of Humor Research* (Berlin and New York, NY, 2008).
2. William Hazlitt, 'On Wit and Humour', in *Lectures on the English Comic Writers* (London and New York, NY, 1963), p. 26.

1 ON LAUGHTER

1. Rather oddly, Ronald de Sousa in *The Rationality of Emotions* (Cambridge, MA, 1987, p. 276) does not regard hysterical laughter as laughter at all.
2. Quoted in Matthew Bevis, *Comedy: A Very Short Introduction* (Oxford, 2013), p. 19.
3. Though Robert R. Provine claims that some of the primates produce laughter-like sounds. See his *Laughter: A Scientific Investigation* (London, 2000), chapter 5. Charles Darwin also believes that monkeys chuckle when they are tickled. See his *The Expression of the Emotions in Man and Animals* (London, 1979), p. 164.
4. Milan Kundera, *The Book of Laughter and Forgetting* (London, 1996), p. 79.
5. See Helmuth Plessner, *Laughing and Crying: A Study of the Limits of Human Behaviour* (Evanston, IL, 1970).
6. I am indebted for some of the above information to Richard Boston, *An Anatomy of Laughter* (London, 1974). For a perceptive potpourri of insights into comedy, see Howard Jacobson, *Seriously Funny* (London, 1997).
7. Immanuel Kant, *Critique of Judgment* (Cambridge, 2002), p. 209.
8. Herbert Spencer, 'The Physiology of Laughter', in *Essays on Education and Kindred Subjects*, intro. Charles W. Eliot (London, 1911), p. 120. A more

recent defence of the relief theory is to be found in J. C. Gregory, *The Nature of Laughter* (London, 1924).

9. See Sigmund Freud, *Jokes and Their Relation to the Unconscious* (London, 1991), p. 167.

10. See Sándor Ferenczi, *Final Contributions to the Problems and Methods of Psychoanalysis* (London, 1955), p. 180.

11. Alexander Bain, *The Emotions and the Will* (3rd edn, New York, NY, 1876), p. 262.

12. Ferenczi, *Final Contributions*, p. 180.

13. See Adam Phillips (ed.), *The Penguin Freud Reader* (London, 2006), p. 563.

14. Bevis, *Comedy*, pp. 24 and 73.

15. Quoted in ibid., p. 29.

16. Simon Critchley, *On Humour* (London and New York, NY, 2002), p. 62.

17. Quoted in ibid., p. 91.

18. Christopher Norris, *William Empson and the Philosophy of Literary Criticism* (London, 1978), p. 86.

19. William Empson, *Some Versions of Pastoral* (London, 1966), p. 114.

20. Thomas Mann, *Doctor Faustus* (London, 1996), p. 378.

21. Charles Baudelaire, *Selected Writings on Art and Literature* (London, 1972), p. 148.

22. Alenka Zupančič, *The Odd One In: On Comedy* (Cambridge, MA, 2008), p. 144.

23. Ibid., p. 144.

24. Quoted by Zupančič, *The Odd One In*, p. 142.

25. Ibid., p. 143.

26. For Dante and comedy, see Giorgio Agamben, *The End of the Poem* (Stanford, CA, 1999), chapter 1.

27. Mikhail Bakhtin, *Rabelais and his World* (Bloomington, IN, 1984), p. 66.

28. Ibid., p. 90.

29. Ibid., pp. 90–91.

30. Ibid., p. 92.

31. Ibid., p. 95.

32. Ibid., p. 84.

33. Ibid., p. 174.

34. George Meredith, *An Essay on Comedy* (New York, NY, and London, 1972), p. 121.

2 SCOFFERS AND MOCKERS

1. See Johan Verberckmoes, 'The Comic and Counter-Reformation in the Spanish Netherlands', in Jan Bremmer and Herman Roodenburg (eds), *A Cultural History of Humour* (Cambridge, 1997), p. 81.

2. See Barry Sanders, *Sudden Glory: Laughter as Subversive History* (Boston, MA, 1995), p. 65. See also Stephen Halliwell, *Greek Laughter* (Cambridge, 2008).

3. See Mary Beard, *Laughter in Ancient Rome* (Berkeley, CA, 2014), p. 33.

4. Thomas Hobbes, *Leviathan* (Cambridge, 2010), p. 43.

5. Donald F. Bond (ed.), *The Spectator* (Oxford, 1965), vol. 1, p. 147.

6. See A. M. Ludovici, *The Secret of Laughter* (London, 1932), p. 31.

7. Anthony Earl of Shaftesbury, *Characteristics of Men, Manners, Opinions, Times Etc* (Bristol, 1995), vol. 1, p. 53.
8. See, for example, Roger Scruton, 'Laughter', in John Morreall (ed.), *The Philosophy of Laughter and Humor* (New York, NY, 1987), who argues that humour lies in a devaluation of the object in question, and F. H. Buckley, *The Morality of Laughter* (Ann Arbor, MI, 2003). Buckley holds that though superiority is not a sufficient condition for laughter, it is always a necessary one. Wordplay, for example, is in his view a competitive affair which signals our intellectual edge over others. For a defence of humour against the superiority thesis, see Ludovici, *The Secret of Laughter*, chapter 2.
9. Quoted by Matthew Bevis, *London Review of Books*, vol. 37, no. 4 (February, 2015), p. 22.
10. Shaftesbury, *Characteristics of Men*, p. 33.
11. Francis Hutcheson, *Reflections upon Laughter, and Remarks upon the Fable of the Bees* (Glasgow, 1750), p. 12. For an account of Hutcheson's benevolistic philosophy, see Terry Eagleton, *Heathcliff and the Great Hunger* (London, 1995), chapter 3.
12. The essay is to be found in Martha Segarra (ed.), *The Portable Cixous* (New York, NY, 2010).
13. Francis Hutcheson, *Thoughts on Laughter* (Bristol, 1989), p. 51.
14. Henri Bergson, *Laughter: An Essay on the Meaning of the Comic* (London, 1935), p. 5.
15. See W. McDougall, *The Group Mind* (New York, NY, 1920), p. 23.
16. See Buckley, *The Morality of Laughter*, p. 37.
17. Arthur Schopenhauer, *The World as Will and Representation* (New York, NY, 1969), vol. 2, pp. 349, 581 and 354.
18. John Willett (ed.), *Brecht on Theatre* (London, 1964), p. 277.
19. Walter Benjamin, *Understanding Brecht* (London, 1973), p. 101.
20. Gillian Rose, *Mourning Becomes the Law: Philosophy and Representation* (Cambridge, 1996), p. 71.
21. John Roberts, *The Necessity of Errors* (London and New York, NY, 2011), p. 204.
22. Sándor Ferenczi, *Final Contributions to the Problems and Methods of Psychoanalysis* (London, 1955), p. 73.
23. See John Lippitt, 'Humour', in David E. Cooper (ed.), *A Companion to Aesthetics* (Oxford, 1992), p. 201.
24. Slavoj Žižek, *Absolute Recoil* (London, 2014), p. 334.
25. George Meredith, *An Essay on Comedy* (New York, NY, and London, 1972), p. 121.

3 INCONGRUITIES

1. For a discussion of these various views, see Christopher P. Wilson, *Jokes: Form, Content, Use and Function* (London and New York, NY, 1979).
2. A psychological account of the theory is to be found in Paul E. McGhee, 'On the Cognitive Origins of Incongruity Humor', in Jeffrey H. Goldstein and Paul E. McGhee (eds), *The Psychology of Humor* (New York, NY, and London, 1972).
3. Noël Carroll, *Humour: A Very Short Introduction* (Oxford, 2014), p. 28.

4. See L. W. Kline, 'The Psychology of Humor', *American Journal of Psychology*, vol. 18 (1907).
5. D. H. Munro, *Argument of Laughter* (Melbourne, 1951), p. 40ff.
6. Thomas Nagel, *Mortal Questions* (Cambridge, 1979), p. 13.
7. See Mary K. Rothbart, 'Incongruity, Problem-Solving and Laughter', in Antony J. Chapman and Hugh C. Foot (eds), *Humor and Laughter: Theory, Research and Applications* (London, 1976).
8. Mark Akenside, *The Pleasures of the Imagination* (Washington, DC, 2000), p. 100.
9. James Beattie, *Essays on Poetry and Music* (Dublin, 1778), vol. 2, p. 366.
10. Ibid., p. 372.
11. Immanuel Kant, *Critique of Judgment* (Cambridge, 2002), p. 210 (translation slightly amended).
12. Herbert Spencer, 'The Physiology of Laughter', in *Essays on Education and Kindred Subjects*, intro. Charles W. Eliot (London, 1911).
13. Charles Darwin, *The Expression of the Emotions in Man and Animals* (London, 1979), p. 200.
14. Robert L. Latta, *The Basic Humor Process* (Berlin and New York, NY, 1999), pp. 39–40.
15. J. Y. T. Greig, *The Psychology of Laughter and Comedy* (New York, NY, 1923), pp. 23–7.
16. Arthur Koestler, *The Act of Creation* (London, 1965), p. 45.
17. John Morreall, *Taking Humor Seriously* (Albany, NY, 1983), chapter 5.
18. Alexander Bain, *The Emotions and the Will* (London, 1875), pp. 282–3.
19. Michael Clark, 'Humor and Incongruity', in John Morreall (ed.), *The Philosophy of Laughter and Humor* (New York, NY, 1987).
20. Max Eastman, *The Enjoyment of Laughter* (London, 1937), p. 27.
21. See Flann O'Brien, *The Best of Myles* (London, 1993), p. 201ff.
22. William Hazlitt, *Lectures on the English Comic Writers* (London and New York, NY, 1963), p. 7.
23. Ibid., p. 9.
24. Ibid., p. 7.
25. Ibid., p. 10.
26. Ibid., p. 27.

4 HUMOUR AND HISTORY

1. See M. A. Screech, *Laughter at the Foot of the Cross* (London, 1997), p. 32.
2. Mikhail Bakhtin, *Rabelais and his World* (Bloomington, IN, 1984), p. 73.
3. See John Morreall (ed.), *The Philosophy of Laughter and Humor* (New York, NY, 1987), p. 228.
4. David Hartley, 'Of Wit and Humour', quoted in ibid., p. 43.
5. George Meredith, *An Essay on Comedy* (New York, NY, and London, 1972), p. 141.
6. Ibid., p. 78.
7. Ibid., p. 118.
8. Ibid., p. 116.
9. See Leah S. Marcuse, *The Politics of Mirth* (Chicago, IL, and London, 1986).

10. Anthony Earl of Shaftesbury, *Characteristics of Men, Manners, Opinions, Times Etc* (Bristol, 1995), vol. 1, p. 65.

11. Keith Thomas, 'The Place of Laughter in Tudor and Stuart England', *Times Literary Supplement* (21 January 1977), p. 81.

12. Quoted in Paul Lauter (ed.), *Theories of Comedy* (New York, NY, 1964), p. 211.

13. John Forster, *The Life and Times of Oliver Goldsmith* (London, 1854), vol. 2, p. 338.

14. Gladys Bryson, *Man and Society: The Scottish Inquiry of the Eighteenth Century* (Princeton, NJ, 1945), pp. 146–7 and 172. See also, for an excellent account of eighteenth-century Scotland, Peter Womack, *Improvement and Romance* (London, 1989). I have drawn in the discussion that follows on some material adapted from my *Crazy John and the Bishop* (Cork, 1998), chapter 3.

15. John Dwyer, *Virtuous Discourse: Sensibility and Community in Late Eighteenth-Century Scotland* (Edinburgh, 1987), p. 39.

16. Adam Ferguson, *An Essay on the History of Civil Society* (Dublin, 1767), p. 53.

17. Bryson, *Man and Society*, p. 27.

18. Henry Brooke, quoted in Thomas Bartlett, *The Fall and Rise of the Irish Nation* (Dublin, 1992), p. 54. For this ideology of so-called commercial humanism, see J. G. A. Pocock, *Virtue, Commerce and History* (Cambridge, 1985).

19. Quoted in Albert O. Hirschman, *The Passions and the Interests* (Princeton, NJ, 1977), p. 90.

20. Katie Trumpener, *Bardic Nationalism* (Princeton, NJ, 1997), p. 76.

21. For Steele's letters to his wife, see Rae Blanchard (ed.), *The Correspondence of Richard Steele* (Oxford, 1941), pp. 208–79.

22. Richard Steele, *The Christian Hero* (Oxford, 1932), p. 77.

23. Shaftesbury, *Characteristics of Men*, p. 45.

24. Francis Hutcheson, *Reflections upon Laughter, and Remarks upon the Fable of the Bees* (Glasgow, 1750), p. 4.

25. Francis Hutcheson, *A Short Introduction to Moral Philosophy* (Glasgow, 1747), p. 18.

26. Francis Hutcheson, *Inquiry Concerning the Original of our Ideas of Virtue or Moral Good* (London, 1726), p. 75.

27. Francis Hutcheson, *Illustrations of the Moral Sense* (Cambridge, MA, 1971), p. 106.

28. Hutcheson, *Inquiry*, p. 257.

29. Ibid., pp. 257–8.

30. See Noël Carroll, *Humour: A Very Short Introduction* (Oxford, 2014), p. 48.

31. Susanne Langer, excerpt from *Feeling and Form*, in Lauter (ed.), *Theories of Comedy*, p. 513.

32. Hutcheson, *Reflections upon Laughter*, p. 37.

33. Elizabeth Carter, quoted by Arthur Hill Cash, *Sterne's Comedy of Moral Sentiments* (Pittsburgh, PA, 1966), p. 55.

34. Quoted by Ann Jessie Van Sant, *Eighteenth-Century Sensibility and the Novel* (Cambridge, 1993), p. 6.

35. Arthur Friedman (ed.), *Collected Works of Oliver Goldsmith* (Oxford, 1966), vol. 1, p. 406.

36. John Mullan, *Sentiment and Sociability: The Language of Feeling in the Eighteenth Century* (Oxford, 1988), p. 146.
37. Lady Morgan, *Memoirs* (London, 1862), vol. 1, p. 431.
38. Harold Nicolson, *The English Sense of Humour* (London, 1956), p. 31.
39. Ibid., p. 23.
40. Matthew Bevis, *Comedy: A Very Short Introduction* (Oxford, 2013), p. 51.
41. Martin Grotjahn, quoted in Lauter (ed.), *Theories of Comedy*, p. 524.
42. See Susan Sontag, 'Notes on Camp', in *A Susan Sontag Reader* (Harmondsworth, 1982).
43. Andrew Stott, *Comedy* (London, 2005), p. 137.
44. Bevis, *Comedy*, p. 3.
45. William Hazlitt, *Lectures on the English Comic Writers* (London and New York, NY, 1963), p. 26.
46. Bevis, *Comedy*, p. 51.

5 THE POLITICS OF HUMOUR

1. Quoted by Matthew Bevis, *Comedy: A Very Short Introduction* (Oxford, 2013), p. 77.
2. Friedrich Nietzsche, *Beyond Good and Evil* (New York, NY, 1966), p. 150.
3. See John Durant and Jonathan Miller (eds), *Laughing Matters* (London, 1988), p. 11.
4. Mary Douglas, *Implicit Meanings* (London and New York, NY, 1999), p. 160.
5. Susan Purdie, *Comedy: The Mastery of Discourse* (Hemel Hempstead, 1993).
6. Noël Carroll, *Humour: A Very Short Introduction* (Oxford, 2014), p. 76.
7. Alenka Zupančič, *The Odd One In: On Comedy* (Cambridge, MA, 2008), p. 217.
8. Konrad Lorenz, *On Aggression* (Abingdon, 2002 [1966]), p. 284.
9. Robert R. Provine argues a somewhat similar case in *Laughter: A Scientific Investigation* (London, 2000), chapter 1.
10. Mikhail Bakhtin, *Rabelais and his World* (Bloomington, IN, 1984), p. 48. Further references to this work will be provided in parentheses after quotations.
11. See Guy G. Stroumsa, *The End of Sacrifice* (Chicago, IL, 2009), p. 82.
12. Enid Welsford, *The Fool: His Social and Literary History* (Gloucester, MA, 1966), p. 200.

INDEX

Book of Solomon 36
Brecht, Bertolt 53–5, 64, 148, 150
Breton, André 43
Brontë, Charlotte 127
Brooke, Henry 106
Brooks, Mel 43
Brothers Karamazov, The (Fyodor
    Dostoevsky) 26
Bryson, Gladys 104, 105
Buchenwald 153
Buckley, F. H. 43, 167 n8
Burke, Edmund 108, 121
Bush, George W. 93
Byron, Lord 126

carnival 31–5, 155–64
    dead levelling and 10
    fantasy revolutions 12
    humour as critique and as Utopia
        155
    imperishable common people of 61
    sense of immortality 96
    sexuality and 19
    superiority theory and 43
Carroll, Noël 138, 139
Carter, Angela 43
Cat in the Hat, The (Dr Seuss) 12
'Catechism of Cliché' (Flann O'Brien)
    84
Chaplin, Charlie 153
Chekhov, Anton 56
Chesterfield, Lord 102
Christian Hero, The (Richard Steele)
    109
Christianity 95, 162–4
Cicero 37, 80, 96, 131
Cixous, Hélène 40
Clark, Michael 72–3
Clinton, Bill 12
Coleridge, Samuel Taylor 117
Columbanus, St 95
Comedians (Trevor Griffiths) 140–57,
    162
    Bert Challenor 140, 145–7
    Eddie Waters 140–5, 147–50,
        152–5, 162
    Ged Murray 140, 141, 146, 148

George McBrain 140, 146, 152–4,
    157
Gethin Price 140–3, 147–54,
    156–7
Mick Connor 140, 145
Mr Patel 154–5
Phil Murray 140, 146, 148, 152
Sammy Samuels 140, 145, 152–4,
    157
'Comic, The' (Ralph Waldo Emerson)
    71
commerce 105–7
community, sense of 103–5
'Comparison between Laughing and
    Sentimental Comedy, A' (Oliver
    Goldsmith) 97
Comus 159
Concluding Unscientific Postscript
    (Søren Kierkegaard) 56
Congreve, William 97, 101–2
Coogan, Steve 63
Country Wife, The (William
    Wycherley) 56
Creation 95
Critchley, Simon 21
Critic as Artist, The (Oscar Wilde) 134
Critique of Judgment (Immanuel Kant)
    10, 69
crying 5–6
Culture and Society 1780–1950
    (Raymond Williams) 151

Darwin, Charles 6, 38, 71, 165 n3
David, Larry 63
De l'esprit des lois (Montesquieu) 107
death 9–10, 18
degradation 158
Dennis, John 97
Descartes, René 3, 115
desublimation 14, 22
Dickens, Charles 83, 119–21, 123–4,
    139
Dictionary of the English Language, A
    (Samuel Johnson) 6
'Difficulty of Defining Comedy, The'
    (Samuel Johnson) 1
Dionysus 10